Religion

in a Free Society

Religion
in a Free Society

by

Sidney Hook

UNIVERSITY OF NEBRASKA PRESS · LINCOLN

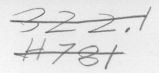

Portions of this book were originally presented in the Montgomery Lectureship on Contemporary Civilization at the University of Nebraska.

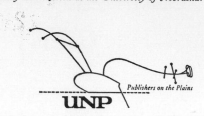

Publishers on the Plains

UNP

Manufactured in the United States of America

For my grandchildren:
Steven, Eric, and Mark

PREFACE

The text of this book was in essentials originally delivered as lectures in the Montgomery Lectureship on Contemporary Civilization at the University of Nebraska, March 23 and 25, 1964. At the time, the country was engaged in a harsh and excited discussion in the wake of the Supreme Court decisions which banned even voluntary prayer and Bible reading in the public schools of the nation. The din and angry echoes have died away: the issues still remain. They are likely to flare up again as the implications of the philosophy of a secular society make themselves felt on the traditional practices and vestiges of religion in public life.

Although I have been a lifelong humanist and secularist, I find it distressing that so many of those who agree with me that religion in a democratic society should be a private matter look to the

Supreme Court to make this view prevail by judicial
fiat, rather than to the outcome of the democratic
process in their local and state communities. For
reasons I try to make clear in the body of these
lectures, I believe this is a shortsighted strategy. It
puts its faith in the wrong place—in the uncertainties
of judicial appointment and the vagaries of judicial
reasoning. In the hope of making immediate gains,
it prejudices the growth of rational sentiments in
the community on which in the long run a healthy
democratic society must rely.

Today the shibboleths of freedom are on every-
body's tongue. But the fact that "freedom" is the
common slogan and rallying cry of groups locked in
political and social combat with each other is evidence enough that a slogan or rallying cry cannot
serve as a substitute for understanding the issues that
divide them. Only an analysis sensitive to the
historical dimensions of the situation we have inherited, and which intelligently unravels the issues
and conflicting interests at stake in the continuing
controversy over the relation between state and
religion, can lead to a satisfactory resolution of the
problem.

The animating idea behind these lectures is that
the American public school is in danger, not because
of the presence or absence of such trivial observance

as prayer or Bible reading, but because of the growing separation between students on the basis of race and religion. The racial separation is *de facto* and not legal, and is an aspect of a complex of problems outside the scope of the present theme. The religious separation of students, where voluntary, is constitutionally valid, and no democrat would dream of challenging its legality. Its educational and political wisdom is another matter, however. The bearing of the Supreme Court's decisions in the field of church-state relations on the *future* of the American public school has not been sufficiently explored. They may be different from what some humanists who have applauded these decisions imagine.

During my stay at Lincoln, Nebraska, I discovered three "national cultural treasures"—to use an expression in vogue in modern Japan—the University of Nebraska, the University of Nebraska State Museum, and the Sheldon Memorial Art Gallery. I am grateful to my hosts, especially to Professor Bernice Slote of the University of Nebraska and Miss Virginia Faulkner of the University of Nebraska Press, for their cordial welcome which made the days of my visit—alas! so few—intellectually interesting, sunny, and gay.

SIDNEY HOOK

South Wardsboro, Vermont

CONTENTS

I. RELIGION IN A FREE SOCIETY   3

II. THE IRRELEVANCE OF SIN   27

III. IS SECULARISM A RELIGION?   43

IV. FROM PRECEPT TO PRACTICE   59

V. MUCH ADO ABOUT PRAYER AND BIBLE READING   77

VI. THE ISSUE OF COERCION   91

INDEX   117

Religion

in a Free Society

I

Religion in a Free Society

The obvious disproportion between the thematic sweep of these lectures and the compass of the discussion may seem curious to some readers. The nature of "religion," the character of "a free society," the meaning of "in" are subjects so vast and complex that one may legitimately question the significance of any observations about them short of an encyclopedic treatise. In addition, one may wonder why a philosopher in this age of Wittgenstein and analysis should concern himself with these problems. Are not empirical matters of this kind outside his ken or beyond his competence?

With respect to this last question, my answer is that we are not dealing with purely empirical questions, and that even if we were, there is a way of approaching them germane to the professional concerns of the philosopher who aims at clarification of issues. The analytic philosopher, once he masters the concrete material, can sort out different kinds of questions that are being asked, and determine what considerations are relevant to what. I go further. The philosophical approach is not merely ancillary or methodological to the pursuit of knowledge in other disciplines. The place of religion in a free society raises questions of *policy*; and at the heart of all major social policies are judgments of value, *normative* judgments of value. One can describe the evaluations people make without being a philosopher. But the evaluation of evaluations is the distinctive task of the philosopher qua philosopher. Whatever else philosophy is or has been in the present or past, the only conception of philosophy which explains the continuity of the philosophic tradition from Socrates to John Dewey, and gives the philosopher a *distinctive* function even if the notion of a distinctive philosophical knowledge is discarded, is that philosophy is the pursuit of wisdom.

As a logician, an analyst of language, a historian of ideas, an epistemologist, a metaphysician, a philosopher may—indeed he must—address himself to other specialists. He has no particular responsibility for making himself intelligible to, or engaging the attention of, others among his fellow men. But if he exercises his distinctive function as a philosopher, then at some point his vision must light up some area of moral concern. A philosopher should have something to say to others who are not professional philosophers, something relevant to their life in its personal or social dimension. I do not believe that this would be denied by Wittgenstein;[1] even if it were, it would be no less valid.

One can discuss religion without any reference to a free society, since men have been religious for a much longer period than they have been politically free. It is doubtful, however, whether one can adequately discuss the nature and problems of a free society without considering the proper role of religion within it. It is differing conceptions of this role which have recently inflamed popular sentiment in the United States and posed some important problems of national and educational policy. These problems go beyond merely questions of nice theoretical distinction. The budgetary allocation of billions of dollars depends upon the view we take of the place of religion in a free society. What is more important, the educational experience of our children in the public schools, and, as we shall see, even in private and parochial schools, will be affected.

It is an illusion—a quaint illusion in the light of

[1] See Norman Malcolm's *Ludwig Wittgenstein: A Memoir* (London: Oxford University Press, 1958), p. 39.

5

RELIGION IN A FREE SOCIETY

the facts—that these questions have been settled by Congress or the Court. It is doubtful whether Congress has the authority, from the point of view of regnant constitutional doctrine, to settle such questions. And although the Court undoubtedly has the authority to do so, this authority unfortunately does not stem from its wisdom in these matters. Ultimately if its authority does not stem from its wisdom, or at least is not buttressed by wisdom, its patent of authority will be eroded.

The nearest thing to a Platonic Board of philosophical guardians in American political life is the United States Supreme Court. But with respect to its opinions on the place of religion and religious practices in American life, few scholars can deny that its judgments have been shifting and confused. Indeed, I believe it is demonstrable that the position of the Court on the key questions of the relation between religion and American political institutions as well as on what constitutes separation of church and state, has been radically incoherent. Even some of its friends admit as much but in Hegelian fashion tend to explain it away, not as an indication of confused thinking, but of a confused objective situation. Thus one enthusiastic admirer of the Warren Court, after deftly exposing "the paradoxes, ambivalences and contradictions" of the Court's decisions, charit-

6

ably concludes that they "are built into the problems" themselves.[2]

This is too convenient a way of dismissing lapses in argument. A hole in a man's understanding does not reflect a hole in his head, no less a hole in existence. Granted that the Court confronts a tangled complex of problems concerning the relation between church and state, the religious and the secular. But the tangle is, to a considerable extent, of its own making, and its tortuous deliberations a consequence of its attempt to rewrite history with every fresh landmark decision. The thinking of the Court could have profited immensely from the analyses of professional philosophers, but unfortunately there has been little of it. As it is, every time a judge is caught in a flagrant contradiction, someone is sure in extenuation to cite the much misunderstood phrase of Justice O. W. Holmes about the life of the law deriving not from logic but from experience. But surely Justice Holmes could not have meant that because something is derived from experience, one cannot make sense of it or give a consistent account of it. His own lifework is a brilliant illustration of rational commentary on, and clarification of, problems arising from experience.

[2] Milton Konvitz, *Expanding Liberties* (New York: Viking Press, 1966), p. 19. This brilliant book often makes better sense of the Court's decisions than the justifying Court opinions.

What makes the existence of a group of philosophic guardians in a democracy tolerable, with the very considerable power that the Supreme Court has, is that its decisions are openly declared, and therefore not immune to the criticism, argument, and discussion of the market place in which one hopefully includes reflective commentary from the academy. Our duty to the Supreme Court as citizens is to obey it and not necessarily to agree with it. In the nature of the case, we shall have to concern ourselves in these lectures with the philosophy and reasoning by which the Court has reached momentous conclusions on matters that touch vital interests to which no intelligent person can be indifferent. How vital these interests are considered is evidenced by the fact that within a few months of the Supreme Court's decision barring any prayer and Bible reading in the public schools more than 147 resolutions had been introduced into the House of Representatives calling for a constitutional amendment to preserve certain practices outlawed by the Court's reading of the First Amendment.

Let us begin by mapping out the relation between religion and a free society on the basis of broad principles of political and social philosophy. What shall we understand by "religion" in our inquiry? As anyone knows who has tried to define "religion" in such a way as to do justice to the way we use the term, it is impossible to find an adequate definition of religion if we are not content with a denotative approach. The nearest thing to the least common denominator of belief in all religions characterized as such is not an article of positive faith. It is rather a negation. It is the proposition that, in Arnold Toynbee's words, "man is not the spiritually highest presence known to man." As soon as we define religion positively as a belief in some presence spiritually higher than man, there is no agreement about what and who it is. There is agreement only that man is not He or It.

This negative and ambiguous proposition is at best only a necessary condition of religious belief. It rules out—properly, I believe—expressions like "the religion of humanity" or "the religion of goodness." It also rules out some of the latter-day popular Japanese cults whose gold-toothed smiling organizers are introduced to visitors as Mr. God, enterprising spirits undoubtedly but not likely to be taken as spiritual presences of any kind—high or low. That belief in this proposition is not a sufficient condition of religious belief is suggested by the consequence that it would automatically give religious standing to spiritualists who populate the cosmos with spiritual beings or presences whose cheerful antics are hardly evidence of religious piety, and sometimes, of plain sobriety. For our purposes, it is enough to identify religion in terms of the familiar denominations organized around a church, whose behavior is differentiated by varied sacral symbols and rituals, and whose credal beliefs acknowledge the existence either of a Supreme Power or an immortal soul or of a cosmic order which is at the same time a moral order, with the corollary that the universe supports our moral ideals and ensures their ultimate triumph.

This question of the definition of religion may turn out to plague us unless we understand it in such a way that "religion" has an intelligible opposite, unless, in short, we know what it means to be nonreligious, and are able to distinguish the non-religious from the religious. If we cannot do this, then it follows that everyone willy-nilly is committed to some kind of religion. One consequence of this is that the attempt to keep religion out of school and government invites the charge that it is a partisan effort to drive out only some specific kinds of religion, allegedly in behalf of the religion of humanism or naturalism or some other particular religious attitude.

The definition of a "free" or "open" or "demo-cratic" society—I shall use these adjectives interchangeably—is not as difficult as the definition of religion, although it, too, has its complexities, happily, not relevant here. It is a society, like our own today, in which the major decisions of government rest ultimately, even if indirectly, upon the freely given consent of a majority of the adult governed. Another way of putting it is that in a free society those responsible for the laws and decisions of government are retained or dismissed depending upon whether or not they are able to elicit the freely given support of the electorate. Consent is freely given *only* where institutional provisions have been made for the free exchange of ideas and where the possibility of political opposition to the existing regime is legally recognized as a permanent feature. Participation in political life is open to all qualified citizens. The principle of majority rule operates in a framework which permits, because of the strategic role of civil liberties, a minority peacefully to become a majority. A genuine democracy is therefore a self-governing community. It permits the winds of doctrine to blow from any quarter. It is opposed to the monopoly, on the part of any private group, and even of the state itself, of the means of communication, publication, and education by which competition in the free market of ideas is carried on and an uncoerced consensus established.

If this, broadly speaking, is what we understand by "religion" and "democracy," what can be reasonably asserted about their doctrinal relationships? And more particularly, what bearing have these relations on developing guidelines in arranging the affairs of church and state in an open society?

1. The first implication to be drawn is that the validity or moral justification of a free or democratic society does not rest, even as a necessary condition, on the belief in any purely religious or theological dogma, or for that matter on any transcendental metaphysical presupposition. A *sufficient* justification of democracy can be found in the empirical consequences—the common fruits of experience—of living together as compared with the consequences of living in a nondemocratic society. Men may offer *supplementary* justification in theological or religious terms for supporting democracy; but unless moral and political values are surreptitiously introduced into the meaning of these terms, no statements which contain them can by themselves serve as either necessary or sufficient conditions for the validity of democracy as a political way of life. One may consistently and fervently believe in the existence of God without believing in democracy. One may consistently and fervently accept the validity of the democratic ideal without believing in God's

existence or immortality or that the cosmic or ontological order is a moral order.

This runs counter to a great deal of modernist folklore as well as to Presidential pieties which assert that democracy is logically based on the Judaeo-Christian tradition, or at least on that part of it which affirms the brotherhood of man under the fatherhood of God. Nonetheless, several lines of consideration reveal that there is no essential connection between democracy and theology. *Analytically*, it is obvious that terms like "brotherhood" and "fatherhood" presuppose that the family is being taken as the model to suggest the proper relation between God and his creatures. But there are families and families. The family is not inherently an illustration of democratic organization. On the contrary, it would serve better as a good paradigmatic case of what is meant by a paternally benevolent than of a free society. The heavenly society is obviously a projection of the patriarchal family. Nor does the term "brotherhood" connote democracy. No one finds it odd that Orwell's tyrant should be called Big Brother.

The historical evidence is as much to the point and even more graphic. Religion is as old as human society; but democracy is of comparatively recent vintage. Judaism and Christianity had a moderating influence on the potential excesses of slavery and feudalism, but we owe the idea of a common humanity, of the basic equality of man, to the Stoic philosophical tradition rather than to the tribal religions which preceded it. It is fashionable to say that the concept of equality before the law, so essential to modern democracy, rests upon the Judaeo-Christian belief that all souls are of infinite importance to God, equally dear in His sight. *Psychologically*, over the centuries when conditions were ripe and men were gropingly formulating the ethical ideal of human equality, the notion that all souls were equal in the sight of God undoubtedly contributed to making the ideal acceptable. But *theologically*, that all souls are equal in the sight of the *Lord*, whether they were souls, in the telling words of Paul, of "bond" or "free" men, was perfectly compatible with the belief in, and practice of, the grossest inequalities before the *law*, not to speak of economic, social, and sexual inequality. The soul of the king and the soul of his lowliest subject are indeed equal before the throne of the Lord. For centuries, however, there was not the slightest difficulty or embarrassment in combining this belief with the belief in the Divine Right of Kings to rule men on earth. Conversely, one may be equal before the law in the City of Man and yet, in some systems of theology,

14

unequal in cosmic status—eternally damned or saved. Conceptions of man's cosmic status undoubtedly in some historical contexts influenced conceptions of men's civic status and vice versa, but logically they are independent of each other.

2. If this analysis is valid, it should be easier to accept my second proposition. Individuals of any religion or no religion at all are entitled to the same rights and privileges as citizens of the democratic commonwealth, provided only that they obey the rules of the democratic "game" or polity. By obedience to such rules is meant the acceptance of certain *prescribed* practices and the avoidance of certain *proscribed* practices. It in no way requires the acceptance of any official ideology or philosophy, whether it be naturalistic or supernaturalistic, as a theoretical justification of such practices. To be a democrat means to act like one; it does not depend upon allegiance to a particular justification of democracy, whether it is Walter Lippmann's "public philosophy" or John Dewey's pragmatism or the religious faith of the Founding Fathers, whatever that faith was.

3. I draw now a conclusion from this of far-reaching significance. In a community in which there are religious differences, and especially in a community like our own of plural religious faiths, religious

belief and observance should be a *private* matter. The state has no responsibility to support religion, no less to establish a religion; no responsibility either to all religions or to any particular one.

The reasons for this conclusion are or should be apparent: (a) Where the state supports one religion over against others, the members of the religions not supported are saddled with extra expense as well as unsought obligations of responsibility for the integrity of religions to which by definition they are indifferent, or even hostile. (b) Where the state supports all religions, it compels those who subscribe to *none* to shoulder the extra expense and unsought obligations for institutions and practices not related to the duties of citizenship or to the health or proper functioning of democracy. The logic behind (a), if valid, is equally compelling for (b); yet some affirm (a) but deny (b).

4. But is this really so? Has not Mr. Justice Douglas proclaimed in *Zorach v. Clauson* that "We are a religious people whose institutions presuppose a Supreme Being"?[3] More significantly, has not the Court in the opinion rendered by Mr. Justice Clark in *Abington Township v. Schempp*—the Bible-reading case—reaffirmed this, and, without a demurrer from any of his brothers, declared that the Court's

[3] 343 U.S. 319 (1952).

judgment gives "specific recognition to the proposition" enunciated by Justice Douglas.[4] Since Justice Brennan in his concurring opinion also endorses unqualifiedly this proposition,[5] a clear majority of the Court is committed to it. This means that Justice Douglas' maxim cannot be dismissed as a mere obiter dictum. It is the considered belief of the Court asserted and reasserted in the face of wide criticism.

Let us examine this belief. If it is true, it undercuts our analysis. More important, it goes a long way towards invalidating the Court's decisions in a whole series of cases including those in which this belief appears as part of the justifying reasons. The pronouncement of Justice Douglas states a historical fact, and then asserts a logical relation. The historical fact is incontestable. Americans are a religious people in terms of church affiliation and attendance at religious services. But that our institutions *presuppose* a Supreme Being is an assertion of an entirely different order.

One would like to know which specific American institution presupposes, or in any way rests upon, the existence of a Supreme Being or belief in Him? Not a single one of the learned Justices tells us. Is it our

[4] 374 U.S. 213 (1963).
[5] *Ibid.*, at 230.

method of nomination and elections? Or our judicial system, including the extraordinary role of the Supreme Court? Is it our practices under our Bill of Rights? Or perchance our system of social welfare or our free enterprise system, to the extent it is free? If a Supreme Being did not exist or belief in Him were lacking, what American institution would lose its foundation or validity? Our federal system, our coinage system, or our system of monogamic marriage? Alas! the Justices preserve a judicial and judicious silence on these crucial questions.

And with good reason! For it is demonstrable that there is no inherent or essential connection between belief or disbelief in the existence of a Supreme Being and any one of the institutions mentioned. To the extent that they rest on good reasons, they are independent of belief in the existence of one Supreme Power, several equally Supreme Powers, or no Supreme Power. To be sure, belief in God has sometimes been conjoined with belief in the validity of these institutions, but it has also been conjoined with belief in the validity of quite different institutions, without any logical or theological inconsistency. After all, Aristotle, and Jehovah, as portrayed in the Old and New Testaments, were the chief authorities of those southerners who penned defenses of the American system of slavery.

Some religious persons have even argued that to seek divine sanction for institutional arrangements which reflect the shifting prudential necessities of human beings in their quest for public order and personal freedom borders on the blasphemous. This would seem to be the view of Karl Barth, who, disregarding the independent authority of moral judgment, used it as a rationalization for refusing to condemn the crimes of Stalinism although he did not fail to castigate severely the Free World for lapses from its ideals.

At any rate, no religion based on a vision of, or belief in, an order of experience transcending nature and history can intelligibly show how the element of the transcendent can function as a *univocal* guide to the choices men face in the temporal and contingent world. Every such derivation is question-begging or circular. "God" has been enrolled under all banners, including those arrayed against each other. Even the recent theological rumor of God's death seems unaccompanied by news of logically associated revolutionary movements in secular life.

The American historical evidence reinforces this conclusion. The early history of religious struggle and conflict reflect not a desire to *extend* the sphere of religious freedom, but rather either an attempt to extend the domination of religious dogma and practices on other sects or an effort to win independence from such domination. There is overwhelming evidence to support Figgis' trenchant observation: "Political liberty is the residuary legatee of ecclesiastical animosities." Religious tolerance has developed not out of love of personal freedom, but more as a consequence of spiritual humility in the quest for understanding first and last things. If anything, the heritage of the religious influence on law is found in a mass of legislation in some of the older states of the Union which offensively invades what may be called the rights of privacy by penalizing socially harmless but unconventional behavior in the area of marriage and divorce, deviant sexual behavior between consenting adults, birth control, and abortion. In addition, religion has inspired legislation against suicide and voluntary euthanasia. When one considers the ocean of tears that have been shed by suffering mankind, especially womankind, because of the inhumanity of laws directly attributable to the influence of religious dogmas, it is hard to find any compensatory consideration. This influence continues into our own day. To the extent that the religious factor can be isolated from other factors of a moral nature in its causal responsibility for any special piece of legislation in the past, that legislation appears today to be of very dubious blessing.

The Supreme Court itself in its bizarre opinion upholding the validity of the Sunday closing laws in several states, legislation originally directly attributable to religious doctrine, offers a justification on purely secular grounds.

We must therefore disagree with the judgment of the distinguished jurists of the Supreme Court. Neither the existence of a Supreme Being nor belief in Him is presupposed by any American institution. Whatever the political organization of Heaven may be, it certainly does not suggest a democratic republic. The fate of Lucifer and lesser rebels shows that there is not even a legally recognized opposition. If the view of the Court is sound, then religion cannot reasonably be regarded as a private matter, but rather one of great public concern.

The most serious aspect of the view I am criticizing is not the purely logical point, but this: If the Court believes that the political institutions of this country depend upon the existence of a Supreme Being or in belief in His existence, then its decisions in the entire series of cases bearing on state and religion become radically incoherent. For if it is true that the validity of our political institutions rest on belief in a Supreme Being, a plausible case could be made for the view that one of the primary functions of our school system, in the interest of good citizenship and patriotism, should be to honor and praise His name. It would be our civic duty as well as a matter of common sense to strengthen belief in Him by all modes of education—public and private. It would mean that we would have to read the First Amendment as forbidding any public support to a *specific* religion at the expense of others, but not as forbidding aid to all religion; precisely the contention of a large group of contemporary religionists agitating for federal aid to parochial schools.

I submit, however, that the Court is clearly in error. By accepting and stressing Justice Douglas' apothegm it has unfortunately confused itself and the country as well. It owes us an explanation of how it is possible to reconcile its decisions on released time, prayer and Bible reading in public schools, and related matters, and the reiterated maxim of Justice Douglas to which it gives "specific recognition." After all, since the founding of the republic some of our institutions have been profoundly modified. They are more democratic today than they were when only white men voted, more democratic than when only men voted, more democratic than when only citizens with high property qualifications voted. At what point did belief or disbelief in the existence of a Supreme Being enter into all this? The evidence is overwhelming that the

causes and grounds which explain the acceptance
of these salutary changes were drawn from an
entirely different set of considerations.

I do not wish to be misunderstood on this point. I
am not asserting that the belief that democracy
presupposes the existence of a Supreme Being by
itself logically *entails* acceptance of a policy by the
state of encouraging and supporting religious
education. Strictly speaking, one may subscribe to
belief in God's existence, and to the view that this
belief is presupposed by the institutions of a free
society, and still maintain that God can look after
His own, and that He requires no aid from school,
society, or government to bring the sheep into the
fold. But in a situation in which education seeks to
nurture the ideals of a free society, a function the
Court recognizes as quite legitimate, then the belief
first articulated by Justice Douglas and then emphat-
ically endorsed by the Court tends to encourage the
adoption of devotional religious exercises and practices of a nonsectarian character precisely along the
lines the Court has condemned.

An analogy will make this clearer. *If* it were
believed that physical exercise during the school day
was essential to preserve the health of students, and
if the school were regarded as properly responsible
for safeguarding the students' health while they were

23

in its care, the natural inference would be that some physical training should be given in school. It would require a showing that some other great value would be violated to make unreasonable the recommendation that some provision for physical education be made in the school curriculum. At the very least, school authorities would be given discretion to make decisions in this regard. It is hardly conceivable that they would be flatly forbidden to carry out the dictates of common sense, lacking any reason to believe that their recommendations prejudice other educational values.

Similarly with respect to the educational bearings of Justice Douglas' momentous but mistaken declaration: *If* faith in a free society, including freedom of religion, rested on some basic religious beliefs, and *if* the schools were considered appropriate agencies to strengthen conviction in the values of a free society, the natural inference would be that some religious education in the schools of the nation would be permissible. It would require a showing that some other basic values would be violated to make unreasonable the recommendation that some religious education be included in the curriculum of the school day. Actually, this line of reasoning, including a variant expression of Justice Douglas' dubious premise, finds explicit statement in one of the great

24

documents of early American history and partly accounts for the stress placed on religious education in the schools of the time. In 1787 Congress declared in the Northwest Ordinance: "Religion, morality and knowledge being necessary to good government and the happiness of mankind, schools and the means of education shall forever be encouraged." In other words, schools should be established in order, among other things, to further religious belief, on the presumed ground that such belief was necessary for good government. There was no fear that the furtherance of religious belief in education was a step towards establishing a church. The Founding Fathers were at least consistent.

A few years ago, in a much publicized address, Chief Justice Warren proposed that in their deliberations leaders in business, labor, education, government, and other areas of social life call in "experts in ethics" to advise them whether or not their proposed decisions were morally right. One may applaud the Chief Justice's insight that basic questions in all these fields have an inescapable moral dimension without necessarily accepting the view that there are "experts in ethics," who can speak authoritatively in fields in which they have not been trained. After all, the Chief Justice made no similar recommendation for the judiciary, despite the fact that there are ethical problems in law as well as in legislation. However that may be, it seems to me that a much better case could be made for the proposal that the Supreme Court consult an expert in logic before it pronounces or publishes its opinions. Although logically consistent thinking does not necessarily lead to truth—there are coherent lies and logical lunatics—logically inconsistent thinking invariably leads to error and confusion at some point. The life of the law is experience; but the wisdom of the law and the justice of the law require that when the law speaks, what it says be ordered in a clear pattern of reasoned discourse which, among other things, permits justified inferences of future judicial behavior. This cannot be done unless there is consistency between the enunciated principles of a judicial opinion and the decision in a specific case, and unless there is some continuity and compatibility in the way principles are applied to similar cases. This consistency has been lacking in the Court's several opinions on matters affecting religion, and sometimes in the very argument of a specific opinion.

II

The Irrelevance of Sin

My main point so far has been that a genuinely democratic state, especially one which contains a plurality of religious faiths, should be neutral in matters of religion, and regard it as essentially a private matter. I shall shortly have something to say about widespread misconceptions of the nature of this neutrality. But, however we construe the notion of neutrality, it is universally admitted that it must be compatible with the phrase in the First Amendment which forbids the establishment of a religion.

The further elaboration of the meaning of neutrality depends upon our understanding of a second main point—perhaps an even more fundamental one—about the place of religion in a free society, viz., that all citizens must be protected in the *free* exercise of their religion. There are two clauses in the First Amendment—one forbidding establishment and one prohibiting interference with the "free exercise" of religion. I believe that it is plausible to interpret the interdiction of an established religion as *one* means of guaranteeing the free exercise of religion. The chief argument against establishment is that it tends to interfere with the free exercise of the religions which are *not* established.

Sometimes this interference of an established religion with the religious freedom of nonestablished religions is direct. More often, in modern times, it is indirect. Paradoxical as it may sound, even the freedom of worship of an established religion may be limited in virtue of the fact that it is an official state religion and therefore subject to state authority on strictly religious matters. Thus, the Church of England cannot revise its own Book of Prayer without the consent of Parliament, which has inherited all the powers of Henry VIII when he set himself up as head of the Church. The odd consequence is that the votes of Jews, Catholics, Atheists, and religious dissenters may be decisive in approving or disapproving the recommendations of the hierarchy of the Church of England about matters affecting the sacred interests of their own communicants. Although there are definite ecclesiastical advantages in enjoying the status of an established religion, from

28

the point of view of religious freedom there are definite dangers, too.

We may take it for granted, then, that the free exercise of religion must take priority over all else in matters concerning religion. Now it may be argued that freedom of religion is a simple corollary of our belief in freedom of speech, press, inquiry, and assembly. Historically, of course, this is not true. Many sects which demanded freedom of religion for themselves (and sometimes for other religious sects) were indifferent to whether or not freedom of speech and press in the *nonreligious* or secular sphere of society was permitted. Their concern was with assuring salvation for themselves in the hereafter, which was dependent upon the free exercise of their religion in this world, rather than with extending the sphere of free inquiry into worldly or strictly political affairs. And conversely, some regimes were more willing to tolerate *religious* freedom than freedom of speech and press outside of religion, although sometimes the two did go hand in hand.

Certainly in our own historical experience, freedom of religion has been supported by our constitutional guarantees of freedom of speech and press. It has also been strengthened by our policy of encouraging the existence and activity of voluntary associations among citizens free to criticize each other as well as the central political authority. The virtue and wisdom of the central political authority in a democracy is and should always be open to question even as its sovereignty in political affairs is acknowledged. But if this is so, is there not revealed a possible conflict between the notion of a government neutral towards religion and the exercise of religious freedom? Suppose the free exercise of one's religion requires adoption of measures for the public good which are not to the liking of members of other religions or of the nonreligious?

For example, suppose a religious group, in the exercise of its religious and political freedom, agitates on grounds which seem good and sufficient to itself for the enactment of laws forbidding divorce or the dissemination of contraceptives or for laws outlawing the consumption of liquor or gambling in any form or for laws prohibiting vivisection and compulsory vaccination. Provided that they conduct their campaign in a lawful manner, it is asked, is it not their right as citizens in a pluralistic society, whatever their religious affiliation be, "to support what they consider good and to criticize what they regard as evil practices"?[1]

[1] V. J. Bourke, *Excerpts from Proceedings of the Annual Judicial Conference of the Tenth Judicial Circuit of the United States, 1963* (St. Paul: West Publishing Co., 1964), p. 70.

Suppose they win a majority through the democratic electoral process and are able to convert their sacramental beliefs into laws binding on all. What happens, then, to the principle of state neutrality? Especially where religion and ethics are intertwined, how are we to prevent the exercise of religious freedom from eroding the practice of state neutrality in matters of religion?

This makes it necessary for us to be a little more precise about the concept of "religious freedom," and to underscore some implications which are overlooked when the phrase is used merely as a slogan. If, when we speak of religious freedom, we mean religious *thought*, then like all thought, its freedom has no other limits than our capacity to think. But where thought is given expression in *words*, and especially in observances and ritual practices, there are obvious limits to such freedom set by the moral standards of the community. Freedom of worship as *behavior* cannot be absolute any more than the other freedoms of the First Amendment, despite Justice Black's stubborn insistence that *all* the freedoms of the Bill of Rights are absolute— even when they obviously conflict with each other.[2]

[2] Cf. my analysis of Justice Black's position, "Lord Monboddo and the Supreme Court," *New Leader*, Vol. XLVI, No. 10 (May 13, 1963), pp. 11 ff.

No community has or can permit complete freedom of religious *practice*. In our own country, despite those who read into the First Amendment an "absolute" right to worship God according to one's conscience, we do not legally tolerate any religious worship which requires human sacrifice or torture, sacred prostitution, or self-immolation. We do not even permit what some observers from different cultures regard as the comparatively harmless and, according to Mark Twain, the occasionally benevolent practice, of plural marriages, despite the behavior of the revered Biblical Patriarchs. Nor do we permit parents on religious grounds to deny their children the rudiments of education or the medical care necessary to preserve their lives.

It follows from all this that in the civil order, *morality must have primacy over all social phenomena, including religion*. Morality is not only autonomous in relation to religion; it is the arbiter of the conflicting moral claims put forth by different religious groups in a pluralistic society.

It is sometimes said in retort to the foregoing that morality itself is derivative from religion. The falsity of this proposition has been established by Plato, Kant, and hosts of modern philosophers. Men build God in their own moral images and attribute their moral discoveries to God in order to give their moral insight greater authority. Nor can they forswear their own responsibility for their moral judgments and actions. Kierkegaard, the great Danish philosopher of religion, used the parable of Abraham and Isaac to illustrate his doctrine of "the teleological suspension of the ethical," and asserted that the highest service to God is *beyond* human conceptions of good and evil, of right and wrong. This may be so in mystical or in existential theology, but not in law or ethics. Men may be absolved in the eyes of God, but they are responsible to other men for any acts of commission or omission whose consequences affect their weal or woe.

Among the fundamental reasons for preserving the neutrality of the state in matters of religion is that religious doctrine and practices have often run counter to the principles of an enlightened morality.[3] To the extent that such religious doctrines and practices have influenced the laws of the state, a conflict sometimes develops between law and morals. For example, today in some jurisdictions in this country, because of the past influence of religion, the law prevents the dissemination of some types of birth control information even to married people; it places great and unreasonable obstacles to divorce

[3] Cf. my *Quest for Being* (New York: St. Martin's Press, 1961), *passim*.

even when there are no children; it penalizes some kinds of therapeutic abortion. In the recent tragic case of a pregnant married woman who had taken thalidomide, even when scientific medical evidence showed that the likelihood was overwhelming that she would give birth to a biological monster, the law, thanks to its religious heritage, ruled out therapeutic abortion as legally possible. In order to avoid committing and helping to compound a crime, the unfortunate woman had to travel to Europe to have the operation performed—an operation which confirmed the fearful prognosis.

The state and its laws, although neutral in matters of religion, cannot be neutral in grave matters of morality.

The independence of morality and religion with respect to theoretical propositions about the nature of the good and right can be established analytically. But the relation between moral behavior and religious education is an empirical question of considerable complexity. Some admit that as a matter of philosophical analysis, religion and morality are independent, for no moral principles or values can be derived from religious or theological statements unless the latter already contain them. They insist, however, like Dr. Robert Hutchins, that "whereas it may be theoretically possible for a man to be good without being religious, it is not practically possible for a man to be good without being religious ... religion is indispensable as a practical matter to the good life."[4]

This sweeping assertion is a gratuitous piece of dogmatism. It flies in the face of the empirical evidence. Despite offhand talk about practical impossibility, all of us know some good men who are not conspicuous for their piety and who have not had a markedly religious early training. Matthew Arnold once observed that conduct is nine-tenths of morality, to which John Dewey added the gloss that habit is ninety-nine one-hundredths of conduct. It is early moral training rather than specifically religious education which plays the greatest role in determining moral character. Any statement about the influence of religious belief on moral practice, once it is admitted that there is no necessary connection between them, is a statement of psychology or social psychology and subject to empirical tests. One can predict the moral behavior of individuals more reliably on the basis of their early and current habits than on the basis of any other factor. There are other factors, to be sure, of which we must take note, especially when children have reached the age of reason. Despite Hume, reason is not altogether

[4] *Morals and Higher Education*, No. 617 (University of Chicago Round Table), January 15, 1950.

the slave of passions. One can teach kindness and truthfulness to the young on the basis of *plural* justifications, the most persuasive of which usually are their consequences in experience.

It is important to recognize the supremacy, or rather the logical priority, of the ethical issue where religious standpoints seem to conflict on a specific question. For unless the question is treated as a *moral* one which invites rational inquiry, what we have is a confrontation of *religious* absolutes, all appealing to some transcendental source, without being able to indicate an objective method by which such differences may be resolved. The moral issue is then befogged by considerations which belong to an entirely different order.

The democratic open society must be neutral to all religious overbeliefs; but no matter how secular it conceives itself to be, it cannot be neutral to moral issues. It seeks to draw these issues into the area of public discussion in the hope that a reasonable consensus may be achieved. So long as the questions of planned parenthood or birth control or therapeutic abortion or voluntary euthanasia are approached from the standpoint of theological doctrine, their resolution is impossible in a pluralistic society of competing theological faiths. Where they are approached as *ethical* questions, the prospects of

36

agreement are much better. If agreement is won on the ethical issue, then, as the history of theological doctrine shows, sometimes changes are made in the meaning and range of applicability of theological dogmas which make certain practices formerly acceptable presently unacceptable, and vice versa.

This enables us to make a distinction that will help us to resolve the problem of the conflict between the concepts of state neutrality and religious freedom. It is a distinction between the freedom to propagate one's religious faith, and the freedom to use the political processes of a democratic society as a convenient strategy to further this faith. Within the limits of the morally permissible, every religious faith is a law unto itself, since membership in it is voluntary, and the burdens it imposes on its members, having been freely accepted, may be freely laid aside without secular sanctions. It can excommunicate recalcitrant individuals from its church, but it cannot excommunicate them from the political community. If a religious group believes that marriage is a sacrament which should never be dissolved by divorce, or that certain foods are taboo because of a Divine command, it may live within the discipline of its faith. But if it seeks to *impose* its conception of marriage or its dietary predilections upon the rest of the community, it is violating the

37

ethos of the open society, and mocks its profession of belief in religious freedom.

The *grounds* on which a position is taken are therefore of the first importance here. Any individual may oppose divorce on moral and social grounds; any individual may seek to extend the pure food laws to certain articles of diet on grounds of public health and welfare. When he does this, he acts as a citizen with a citizen's right to be wrong, and not as a member of a disciplined religious group voting to make his particular religious dogma binding upon others. He presumably is open to argument and evidence of an empirical kind. It is one thing to advocate prohibition of the manufacture and sale of alcohol, and a ban against national lotteries, on the ground that such legislation furthers the public welfare. Individuals of all religious faiths or none may subscribe to the proposal. But it is something else again to propose that gambling and the consumption of liquor should be forbidden by law because they are *sinful* according to some religious dogmas. A democratic community may recognize— indeed, it must recognize—what is morally evil, but it cannot recognize the category of sin, legislate against it, and punish those for whom the proscribed action is not sinful. One man's sin may be another man's duty and a third man's bliss. Even if a religious group commands a majority in a democratic community, it has no justification, according to the spirit of democratic polity, to legislate against sin. Such action is an invitation to religious civil war. Usually when there is sufficient evidence that something is evil or socially undesirable to a point where legal action seems indicated, it is unnecessary to introduce theological dogma to support proposals to cope with it. It is only when persuasive moral argument is lacking or when, as in the case of therapeutic abortion and some other measures of birth control, the moral argument for the practice is overwhelmingly cogent, that recourse is made to theological dogma. But in a community of plural and incompatible religious faiths, at any point where a theological dogma is introduced to control public policy, it is a dagger thrust at the very heart of the political democratic process.

This position expressed in a public lecture and reported in the press caused an outcry in some Catholic circles on the ground that refusal to proscribe as illegal actions that are sinful "encourage social anarchy."[5] Are not "murder, bank robbery and rape sins?" it was asked. This criticism is based

[5] Cf. Rev. Hugh Morley, O.F.M. Cap., "Sin and Professor Hook," *Catholic News* (archdiocesan publication of New York), December 1, 1962.

on an elementary confusion between moral evil, or
crime, and sin. It may be that all morally evil or
criminal acts are sinful—this is a nice point in
sacred theology—but not all sinful actions are morally evil or criminal. It is because we share certain
objective standards of morality that we avoid
social anarchy, and not because we share certain
standards of what is sinful. If slavery is wrong,
it is not because it is sinful, but because it is morally
evil. If Abraham had refused to listen to the voice
of Jehovah, his act would have been sinful. Had he
actually carried out Jehovah's command, his act
would have been morally evil and criminal. It may
be sinful to violate the Commandments of the
Decalogue—but sinning against the injunctions not
to murder or bear false witness is a moral crime,
whereas sinning against the injunction not to covet
one's neighbor's wife (or husband) is at most an
imprudence and should never be treated as a crime,
while violating the Sabbath as such is not even an
imprudence and in any case should concern no one
but the person involved. To equate all of these
violations as equally evil because they are equally
sinful is to be deficient in moral sensibility. That is
why, among other reasons, the state cannot recognize any category of sin.

Does this position entail, under the guise of state

neutrality, a hostility to religion, a doctrinaire secularism which is just as foreign to freedom of religion as is theocracy? This is often asserted; but is it true? Does this position justify recent Supreme Court decisions with respect to religion in the public schools and public life? Does it *entail* any practical corollaries? These questions we shall now examine.

III

Is Secularism a Religion?

So far, I have tried to develop in a broad way what the role of the state or government of a free society should be towards religion, especially in a community of plural faiths. I have argued for the validity of a secular approach which, pledged to uphold freedom of religious worship as well as freedom not to worship, imposes the responsibility of strict neutrality upon the state or government. For historical reasons which at the moment it is unnecessary to enter into, the attitude of the American state from the time of its founding to the present has *not* been one of neutrality towards religion. There has never been a wall of separation between church and state in America, although it is true that efforts to build such a wall have been made and have been crowned with a modest success. To deny the historical facts is productive only of confusion. There is no evidence

43

that the enlightened philosophy of Jefferson and Madison with respect to relations of the state to religion was shared by a majority of their legislative contemporaries.

Leaving the historical facts aside, I am defending the Jeffersonian ideal of separation on political, democratic grounds, which was only an ideal in Jefferson's time as well. I wish to address myself to the oft-repeated assertion that this ideal of separation is an expression of a secularism that is hostile to the free exercise of religion. There is one superficially plausible ground for believing this to be true. If historical practices have developed which are incompatible with separation, then if we approve of the ideal of separation, we must in principle condemn these practices—even if for a variety of reasons we do not proceed to abolish them by legislative decree. But it would be a mistake to interpret the condemnation of these historical practices, say like tax exemption of church property, payment of salary for army chaplains, special provision for exemption from military duty on religious grounds, as evidence of hostility to religion. For that would be begging the question at issue, which is: should the wall of separation have been breached in the first place? Or, to particularize, is the request that churches pay for the tax-supported services they enjoy an expression of secular hostility to religion?

Before judging whether secularism is hostile to religion because of its presumed impact on present religious practices, let us look more closely at the secularist position. The secularist holds that the public or civic order, whether it affects military, education, or fiscal affairs, must not be invaded by any religious group for purposes of partisan advantage. If the state is truly neutral, then no privilege can be extended to any religious group which is not open to any nonreligious group. Why should this view be regarded as itself an objectionable invasion of the civic order by a sectarian philosophy hostile to religion? Not only have some theologians charged that it is not "true neutrality" to proclaim the state neutral to all religion; Supreme Court justices have also expressed a fear lest some conceptions of neutrality mask "a passive or even active hostility to the religious." Thus Mr. Justice Goldberg, in his concurring opinion on the Bible-reading cases, wrote:

> It is said, and I agree, that the attitude of the state toward religion must be one of neutrality. But untutored devotion to the concept of neutrality can lead to invocation or approval of results which partake not simply of that noninterference and noninvolvement with the religious which the Constitution commands,

45

but of a brooding and pervasive devotion to the secular and a passive, or even active, hostility to the religious. Such results are not only not compelled by the Constitution, but, it seems to me, are prohibited by it.[1]

It is a pity that Justice Goldberg left unexplained the difference between an "untutored," bad devotion to the concept of neutrality and a tutored, good devotion, aside from saying that the untutored devotion to the concept of neutrality leads to results prohibited by the Constitution. It would have been instructive to learn who is to tutor us properly, so that we could distinguish between devotion to the concept of neutrality and devotion to the secular. Further, is it only "brooding and pervasive" devotion to the secular which is objectionable? What of a frenetic and intermittent devotion, and how shall we distinguish between them? The rhetoric of the quoted passage masks a failure to show in what specific way devotion to the secular implies hostility to religion. After all, some religious thinkers, whose lives attest to their piety, have been advocates of a secular society. Nor does Justice Goldberg or any other critic of the secular attitude offer evidence to convince us that in historical fact such an attitude has weakened the place of religion in American life.

[1] *School District of Abington v. Schempp,* 374 U.S. 306 (1963).

46

The decline of religious orthodoxy cannot straightaway be equated with the decline of religion. Whatever changes have taken place in the *content* of religious doctrine are more readily attributable to the impact of scientific knowledge on religious dogma than to growth of a secular sentiment hostile to religion.

A characteristic semantic ploy is observable in the discussions of the secular attitude by critics who regard it as inherently hostile to the practice of religion in personal or private life. The term "secular" becomes transmuted into "secularism." It is then prefaced with the adjective "sectarian." Before long, sectarian secularism is represented as a militant, crusading atheism which seeks not merely to uphold the public and civil order against invasion by religious groups for partisan advantage—the only reason for building a wall of separation between church and state—but as engaged in an unremitting campaign to drive religion out of society altogether. The final twist is to charge that *au fond* secularism is itself a religion that under the guise of neutrality seeks to establish its own sectarian hegemony over public life.

This bizarre misconception which takes many variant forms overlooks the simple fact that secularism is a political theory about how church and state should be related in society, and that among its supporters can be found both the religious and the irreligious. In passing we should observe that secularism and religious faith are *logically* independent of each other. Not only are some religious individuals secularists, some irreligious and nonreligious individuals, e.g., Napoleon and Metternich, have been strong supporters of an established religion. Even a philosopher like George Santayana, for whom religion was a set of morally edifying fairy tales, had no objections to an established church.

Whoever the secularists in American life are, a decent respect for the facts of American history should acquit them of the charge that they have been successful in undermining religious faith or sentiment in American life. The influence of religion in American society has grown very markedly despite the fact that certain religious observances in the public order have been curtailed or have suffered gradual evanescence from the time the Constitution was adopted to the present. Whatever the *quality* may be of the present-day religious revival or renaissance in American life, its scope or pervasiveness can hardly be called into question. The God of the Pilgrim Fathers is no longer worshiped, but surely a belief in hell-fire, brimstone, and the eternal dam-

48

nation of the unbaptized is not a *sine qua non* of genuine religious faith. Americans may no longer riot or stone one another over points of theology; but religion has become more of a folk phenomenon, indifference to, or defiance of which, is considered a mark of eccentricity or a breach of good manners. It is hardly an exaggeration to say that in America today it would be more difficult for an outspoken atheist like Robert Ingersoll to become President than for a Catholic, a Jew, a woman, or a God-fearing Negro. Although it annoys certain staid and respectable elements in our population to be reminded of it, the fact is that it was possible in the nineteenth century for Robert Ingersoll to nominate James G. Blaine for the Presidency at a national convention of the Republican party. This would hardly be possible today for Ingersoll's spiritual descendants—a fact that may be taken as a gauge of the religious temper of the American people.

The very growth in religious feeling—which makes up in diffusiveness for what it lacks in intensity—as well as in religious writing and denominational affiliation bespeak not a retreat before an irreligious secular offensive, but potentially an increase of public pressures on the public order to accommodate itself to the phenomenon of religious growth.

It is awareness among the religious and nonreligious alike that differences in religious belief, if they obtrude into the public order, as they unfortunately have, may become focal points of religious and moral conflict, which has led to the assertion of the principle of religious neutrality on the part of the democratic state. Whether or not this is merely a reassertion of a principle accepted during the founding years of the republic, i.e., whether the secularist philosophy of Jefferson and Madison was the canonic guide at the time the Constitution was adopted, we shall not now consider. For it is an open question whether Jefferson and Madison were complete secularists. One may be opposed to an established church without believing that the state should be neutral in all religious matters. Whether the principle of religious neutrality, proclaimed on occasion by the Supreme Court, represents a constitutional innovation or whether it is a plain reading of a plain text, we shall leave moot for the moment. Suffice it to say here that, judging by the twisting and turning and doubling back of the Court decisions, if we are dealing with a plain text, it might just as well have been written in Etruscan. But whether the principle of religious neutrality expresses the *wisdom* of a democratic polity in a community of plural religious faiths, of that there can be no reasonable doubt.

50

Nonetheless it is doubted. And before we can deny that the doubt is reasonable, we must consider the reason for the doubt. The main reason given is that a consistent secularism, departing from the view that church and state should be neutral, must end up with a view that makes an idol of the state, in short ends up with a substitute religion. Professor Will Herberg, among others, speaks of "the idolatrous civic religion of Americanism" as a consequence of the affirmation of the principle of neutrality. Worship of the state—of any state, it is alleged—is a form of totalitarianism, which, if not as extreme as Fascism or Communism, belongs to the same genus. This criticism is directed especially against those secularists who have rather misguidedly spoken of "the religion of democracy" and are in consequence taxed with having substituted the worship of the state for the worship of God.

If we understand by "democracy" a political system in which the freely given consent of the population is ultimately decisive, and in which there is an unwavering allegiance to the institutions and values that make such consent possible, e.g., a free market in ideas, then I believe it can be shown that the above criticism is invalid. Actually, the democratic state is not an object or, in the first instance, a *power*, but a set of processes that enable us

51

to derive a common public policy from conflicting public opinions.

Although it has its rites and symbols, the democratic state does not command the total or even the supreme allegiance of anyone. Within the limits of public *morality*, it permits individuals to worship at any private altar. Within the limits of public *order*, and the necessities of public welfare, limits which cannot be repudiated except by anarchists, it acknowledges the legitimacy of plural authorities. It therefore has no party line in science whether it be astronomy or zoology, in art or music, philosophy or theology, or any other theoretical discipline. Those who see in secularism a mask of latter-day Jacobinism or Bolshevism are terrorizing themselves by fancies born of historical ignorance and defective logic. It is simply false to say of democratic secularists that they make "all authority which does not reside in the state an opponent of the well-being of the body politic." The family, the church, the school, the trade union, the professional association are all recognized as sources of authority in a democratic community. The area of their competence is freely acknowledged. It is only when the authority of a private association seeks to usurp public authority, and exploit the agencies of the state to hold the allegiance of its adult members or to impose that allegiance on others, that the democratic state intervenes. The persecution of religion by Communist states is a consequence *not* of their secularism, but of their political and cultural dictatorship.

A secular democracy like our own honors a man's religious faith to a point where it is prepared to exempt him from the performance of certain duties owing to the state, like combatant military service, if he sincerely finds such service incompatible with his religious conscience. Strict neutrality requires that the same exemption be extended to the conscience of the nonreligious as well. But the extent to which the state has been willing to go to meet the conscientious religious scruples of its citizens is evidence of how recondite and farfetched is the indictment of the religionist that under secularism the state becomes an all-devouring Moloch.

The enlightened secularist regards public or political life as far from being the only or most important dimension of life. It constitutes only a small part of what Santayana calls "natural society." Its greatest virtue is to provide the conditions for "free society" and "ideal society," those pastures of the spirit in which in voluntary companionship men cultivate their interests in art, science, and religion. When a secularist says that religion is a private matter, we must remember that for him, as for any other

53

reflective person, the private is a vast realm which the public life of a democracy defends against arbitrary incursion. The greater the interdependence among us, enforced by the consequences of growth in technology and population, the more precious does the private and personal become. No democratic secularist or humanist seeks, for example, to give the state a monopoly of the processes of education. At most, the state can require that certain minimum standards of literacy, of skills and information be upheld. Any other education may be given by private agencies, including the church. But no private agency has a claim upon the state to underwrite its program of instruction.

As a secularist, I can appreciate and reaffirm the last words uttered by Edith Cavell before a firing squad during the First World War: "Patriotism is not enough." Nor is any brand of theology or religion enough. In this world, of nothing can it be said that it is enough. Patriotism is one value among others, and in the moral economy where right conflicts with right, good with good, and the right with the good, some other value may transcend it. The children who, out of a misguided sense of patriotism, betrayed their parents as secret enemies of the state to the authorities in Nazi Germany or the Soviet Union or Communist China were tearing

a rent in the texture of intimate personal relationships much graver than any derelictions against the
state of which their parents may have been guilty.
A secular democracy worthy of the name would
never demand that a child surrender his soul or
his moral integrity to the state.

There remains to consider the question whether
the justifiable limits of religious freedom in a secular
state constitute undue interference with religion.
These justifiable limits flow from legislation inspired by concern with the public welfare which
either prescribes certain practices like compulsory
schooling or vaccination, or proscribes other practices like plural marriages or the employment of
minors. Suppose a bill were introduced into the
legislature of a democratic community regulating in
the interests of prevention of cruelty to animals the
mode of their slaughter in meat-processing plants.
This conceivably might conflict with the practices of
ritual slaughter prescribed by some religious sects.
The consideration would be relevant in determining
whether the legislation should be adopted. If,
however, the representatives of the community regarded the *moral* issue as of overriding concern, and
if the legislation were adopted on moral grounds, all
citizens, whatever their religion, would be bound by
it. So long as the legislation was aimed at certain

immoral practices, any disability suffered by individuals because of their religious beliefs would have
to be borne by those affected. They would retain, of
course, their political right to agitate for the abolition of the law in question; but like the unrecon-
structed Mormons, so long as the law remained in
force they would have to suffer the cross of monog-
amy or suffer in jail.

Difficult cases would arise in situations where the
law would normally prosecute for false representation or fraud if these were made in a nonreligious
context. Wilhelm Reich, for example, ran afoul of
the law because he sold an orgone box to sufferers
from cancer after the Pure Food and Drug Administration declared that there was no scientific warrant
for asserting that these contraptions had any therapeutic effect. Had Reich been a founder of a
religious cult and offered his orgone box to communicants with the assurance that the Lord would
guarantee heavenly bliss to those who lay in it with
genuine religious faith, he would have been beyond
the reach of the law. In a secular society the courts
cannot punish for fraud in matters of religious belief.
If they did, they would have to take a position on
what is true or false in religion, which is beyond their
competence and authority. If the members of his
flock choose to sign over all their earthly possessions

to Father Divine in exchange for a much richer heavenly portion, they are not engaging in an ordinary commercial transaction. An action sanctioned or inspired by religious belief, provided it is not itself legally proscribed on independent grounds, is constitutionally privileged. If it is punishable, it is because it is prejudicial to the public welfare, and not because it is religious.

Any attempt to enforce the statutes against fraud and misrepresentation where religious belief is concerned would produce widespread chaos and fear of religious persecution.[2] The criteria of scientific truth are obviously unacceptable to the religious mind as criteria of religious truth. Whatever the criteria of religious truth are, from the standpoint of any particular religion, either some of the dogmas of every other religion are false or the entire set of its dogmas is insufficient. A secular state that imposed scientific criteria of truth on religious representations that promised salvation in exchange for the surrender of earthly goods or the performance of personal services would be guilty of intolerance and bigotry. This would be secularism run amok.

Actually, where the public order and public

[2] Cf. the interesting discussion by Jonathan Weiss in "Privilege, Posture, and Protection 'Religion' in the Law," 73 *Yale Law Journal*, 593 (1964).

morals are not threatened, a secular state that professes to be guided by the scientific spirit would be hospitable to the widest variety of beliefs, since it eschews the notion of absolute truth and relies on the critical methods of inquiry to expose error. It has no need to compel or coerce belief, because it recognizes the right to err as integral to the very process by which scientific truth is established. On the other hand, those religions which accept the Augustinian dictum that where the truth is known, there is no right to err, and combine this with the conceit that they have been vouchsafed an infallible revelation about the nature of human destiny, are already predisposed to an attitude of self-righteous intolerance.

Some critics of secularism have called upon "secular liberals to resist the totalitarian temptation to which they so often seem to be succumbing," and imply that the secular vision of a good society threatens to "systematically exclude the protest of religion" against current evils.[3] But no documentation has been offered to show that any serious secularist thinker holds views even remotely approximating this position. It is merely a caricature that stalks the imagination of the critics of a secular culture.

[3] Cf. William Clancy in *Religion and the Free Society* (New York, 1958), p. 32.

58

IV

From Precept to Practice

At the time the American republic was founded, it had gone further than any other contemporary nation in separating the state officially from any religion. What this meant particularly was that the national government repudiated the entire notion of an established church on the federal level and that it refused to recognize the profession of any religious belief or the practice of any religious observance as a condition of political rights. Nonetheless, despite this progressive step it was notorious that the American people were strongly religious in outlook. Almost all European observers commented on this, usually with some asperity. Even the young Karl Marx, who knew little about conditions in America, writing in 1844 on the basis of his familiarity with the works of Beaumont, de Tocqueville, and Hamilton, refers to America as "peculiarly the land of religiosity."

Under the circumstances, it is hardly surprising that the American republic in its early years was not committed to a thoroughgoing secularism or complete neutrality in religious matters. It was not even committed to democracy as we understand it today. Nor is this a reason for embarrassment or shame, since at the time the emerging American nation, despite the disgrace of slavery as an institution, was far in the lead of the concert of nations in its defense of the rights of man.

It is one thing on the basis of pure democratic principles to develop a scheme in which religion is a private matter in every respect. It is quite another to expect these principles to operate outside a historical context. We cannot escape history. Our theoretical principles must function today not as if we were creating institutions *de novo*, but as principles of revision and reform of ongoing forms of life.

These considerations are pertinent to the entire range of practical issues involving church and state that have agitated the country for at least a generation. Several volumes could be devoted to these issues, particularly if we are concerned not with what is wise and desirable from a democratic point of view, but with what is *constitutional*. In view of the periodical preoccupation of the nation with what is constitutional or not, it cannot be emphasized too often and too strongly that what is wise and what is constitutional are not necessarily the same things. As a rule, however, those who deem any particular piece of legislation constitutional strive mightily to show that it is wise, and vice versa. The slightest familiarity with the history of the Supreme Court should establish the validity of the distinction between what is wise and what is constitutional as beyond reasonable doubt. Measures in the past declared clearly constitutional were unwise, and measures that appeared clearly wise were declared unconstitutional. The obvious truth is that no one knows what the key words and phrases of the Constitution mean until the Court declares their meaning, and what the Court declares depends on the current political philosophy of those who are appointed to the bench. Appointments only too often are repayments of a political debt rather than recognition of outstanding judicial learning and merit.

It is hard enough to believe that the words of the Constitution are clear in view of the many split decisions on questions of critical importance. It is even harder to understand how words whose meanings have been fixed by judicial fiat, once a conflict has arisen and been resolved, can again bear the weight of incompatible interpretations.

After all, the words of the First and the Fourteenth Amendments were the same in 1883, in 1896, and in 1954. Yet in 1883 they lent themselves to the nullification of the Civil Rights Acts of 1875, which outlawed racial discrimination in public places;[1] and in 1896 to the proclamation of *Plessy v. Ferguson*,[2] which by sanctioning separate and equal facilities for white and black riveted the yoke of segregation on the necks of Negro citizens in the South; and in 1954 to the memorable decision of *Brown v. Topeka Board of Education*,[3] which reversed the previous decision on the weak ground that separate facilities were *inherently* unequal (are none but coeducational schools therefore unconstitutional?) and on dubious and irrelevant psychological evidence, instead of on the overwhelmingly strong grounds expressed in the dissenting opinion of the first Justice Harlan in the civil rights case of 1883.

Since the same set of words cannot in the same legal context have these incompatible meanings, we must look beyond them for the clues on how to read

[1] See the illuminating discussion of these cases in M. R. Konvitz's *The Constitution and Civil Rights* (New York: Columbia University Press, 1947), and M. R. Konvitz and T. Leskes, *A Century of Civil Rights* (New York: Columbia University Press, 1961).

[2] 163 U.S. 537 (1896).

[3] 347 U.S. 483 (1954).

them. We must conclude that the expressions of the Constitution invoked in these and similar cases are propositional functions whose specific meanings are legislated into them by whichever group of judges happens to occupy the bench. In this process of legislation even the influence of the judges' law clerks is not to be discounted. This tendency towards judicial legislation is aggravated at a time when judicial activism is running wild, and, on questions of state and religion, in various directions at once. If the doctrine of *stare decisis* played as little a role in the field of civil and criminal law as it plays today in constitutional law, the country would be in a state of legal chaos. Since what one Court can do, another can undo, in the long run it seems to me that those who wish to keep religion out of the public life of a free society should look primarily to the educational processes of democracy itself rather than to the decrees of the Court to strengthen and extend the secular position.

If we approach the problem of church and state relations from the standpoint of what is required by the logic, ethics, and civic health of a democracy, we can avoid two practices that make Supreme Court decisions such tortured exercises in rationalization. The first is the attempt to read into the text of the Constitution what democratic sense *today* prescribes as just and reasonable, despite the evidence that the democratic philosophy, particularly its belief that the tyrannies of minorities are more to be feared than the tyranny of the majority, was not widely prevalent. Jefferson was more the prophet of future democratic thought than the exemplar of current political thought. Nonetheless, Mr. Justice Clark asserts, as if there were no question about it, that "the views of Madison and Jefferson, preceded by Roger Williams, came to be incorporated not only in the Federal Constitution but likewise in most of our States."[4] If "most" means a majority, it certainly was not true at the time the federal Constitution was adopted, since most of the states had established churches. Although the Founding Fathers believed in God and that man's inalienable rights were rooted in Him, it is not true to say, as Justice Clark does, that this belief is "evidenced in their writings from the Mayflower Compact to the Constitution itself." The Constitution, as distinct from the Declaration of Independence, contains no reference to God whatsoever.

This arbitrary exegesis of the text of the Constitution and wishful mind reading of its authors is usually accompanied by a second and allied error. In order to fortify a position which is warranted by

[4] *Abington School District v. Schempp*, 374 U.S. 203 (1963).

64

our *current* democratic ethos, historical reconstruc-
tion of the past is undertaken that does intellectual
violence to the facts of past institutional life. A
phrase, a sentence, or a passing reference of Jefferson
or Madison is seized upon to prove that the Justice's
current reading of the Constitution is nothing but a
transcription of the intent of the Founding Fathers—
a feat of mind reading all the more impressive because some of the practices currently condemned
were never even considered at the time the Constitution was adopted, while some of the practices then
in vogue cast doubt on the validity of the mind
reading. What the Founding Fathers would have
thought and done *if* they were twentieth-century
democrats is a question quite distinct from what
they actually thought and did as eighteenth-century
liberals and republicans. They obviously were not
legislating *for* the states when they forbade the
establishment of a religion for the nation. On the
contrary, they were adopting a self-denying ordinance pledging not to interfere with the religious
freedom of the states, in most of which established
churches were found. In all likelihood, the Constitution would not have been adopted if the states
believed that *their* freedom of religious practice
would be curtailed. The established state churches
fell into desuetude not because of the operation of

federal law or the sword of the nation, but in virtue of the uncoerced growth of democratic sentiment. This was true not only for the established churches in the states, but for other manifestations of religion in public life. The interdiction of an established religion in national life was motivated at the time primarily by the belief that an established church threatened religious freedom, not because of any lukewarmness toward the public role of a non-established religion in public life. One graphic detail can summarize a volume of evidence. Immediately after adopting the Conference Committee's report on the First Amendment, a group of legislators was appointed to wait on the President of the United States to petition that he recommend to the people a day of public thanksgiving and prayer. Those who approved this and similar measures would have been bewildered had they been told that the intent of the First Amendment was to build a high and impregnable wall of separation between religion and the state.

We are assured, however, by all the Justices that the line to be drawn between what is permissible and impermissible in the way of involvement of religion in public life is to be derived not from what is required by contemporary democratic theory, but from the historical facts of the past, and particularly

66

the minds of the founders of the republic. Thus Mr. Justice Brennan in his concurring opinion in the Bible-reading cases tells us: "I believe that the line we must draw between the permissible and the impermissible is one which accords with history and faithfully reflects the understanding of the Founding Fathers."[5]

If Justice Brennan is serious about the use of these criteria, then he would be hard put to explain why the historical religious practices which obtained in 1789 would be unconstitutional in 1963. And although there were no public schools then on the order of our own today, surely what we know of the history and understanding of the Founding Fathers justifies the belief that they would have swallowed prayer and Bible reading, to which they were prone on many public occasions, without the slightest constitutional embarrassment. Is it not simply absurd to say that an interpretation based on the Fourteenth Amendment, adopted some 75 years after the Constitution came into effect and applied to the states some 150 years after that event, reflects the understanding of the Founding Fathers?

That the U.S. Supreme Court has no warrant in the *text* of the First Amendment to rule as it has on some of the issues which have come before it

[5] *Ibid.*

involving the payment of tax money to parochial
schools or providing for the religious education of
students on released time is manifest in the weird
pattern of its decisions and by what the Justices say
to each other about it. Thus after ruling in *McCollum
v. Board of Education*[6] that a tax-supported public
school could not permit religious groups to give
religious education to students on school premises,
it ruled in *Zorach v. Clauson*[7] that if such instruction
were given off the school premises but still on school
time with students as captive audience, this would
not be a breach of the wall of separation. Presumably, religious instruction in school buildings consumes tax money as a proportionate share of the
overhead. Religious instruction off school premises
consumes no tax money. Now, if the difference
between *McCollum* and *Zorach* centered only on the
use of tax money to further religious purposes, then
the tax exemption of churches and religious founda-
tions as well as the payment of salaries of military
chaplains are clearly unconstitutional. Prayer reciting and Bible reading could hardly be invalidated
on the ground that they involved expenditure of
tax money for religious purposes. On the other hand,
if what is objectionable in the practice of released

[6] 333 U.S. 203 (1948).
[7] 343 U.S. 306 (1952).

68

time for religious instruction is that the public school is furthering a religious purpose regardless of its cost, then it matters little whether religious instruction is given on or off school premises during normal school time. This inconsistency led Mr. Justice Jackson, dissenting in *Zorach v. Clauson*, to write: "Today's judgment will be more interesting to students of psychology and of the judicial process than to students of constitutional law."[8] Nothing one could say of the Court could more awesomely sap our confidence in its adherence to objective and neutral principles of interpretation.

As democrats and secularists, we must place greater reliance upon education than on the shifting majorities of the Supreme Court to keep the state neutral in matters of religion. A wise political strategy would concentrate on the large issues that go directly to the heart of the problem, like tax exemption for churches, rather than on peripheral questions like noncompulsory Bible reading in schools. Resort to court action is justified when proposals are adopted which would introduce *new* measures, or restore old ones, of religious prescription in public life, especially into public education, or which would divert public tax monies to the support of parochial schools. But where we are

[8] *Id.* at 314.

69

dealing with vestigial religious practices of a non-compulsory nature that have been in existence for a century or more with or without the blessings of the First Amendment (because they have never been challenged), practices that have lost their sectarian character and involve minimal or no public outlays of money, I would let sleeping legal dogs lie.

With respect to the first class of phenomena, the duty of the Court is plain. It must veto any measures to bring the state into the picture as sponsor or supporter of any religious activity, since this would lead to a proliferation of demands for greater involvement.

With respect to the second class of phenomena, were we starting from historical scratch, I would urge a careful scrutiny of all aspects of political and educational life in order to eliminate references to religious ideas and practices in all forms of public ritual. Were we starting anew as a modern democracy, there would be no justification for the mention of God in the national anthem, in oaths of any kind, in the uncoerced use of prayer or Bible reading, or the use of the device "In God We Trust" on the national currency. Dropping this last slogan would be in accordance not only with the attitude of aseptic neutrality, but in the interest of religion itself. Since one of the most sacred texts of the Western religious tradition proclaims that "the love of money is the root of all evil," one would imagine that the sensibilities of the truly pious would be outraged by the stamping of this device on the currency they use, since it suggests the worship of mammon.

But with respect to these ritualistic linguistic uses, we are *not* starting from historic scratch. They have become so much a part of folklore that few if any individuals are upset by their continued employment. Before throwing a community into turmoil which is the result of legally prohibiting an innocuous practice to which many have been accustomed, one should ask the common sense questions: "Who is being hurt by it? What important social need requires its abolition? Why the urgency of dispelling the faint aroma of early religion from the social atmosphere?"

Where the presence of religion makes a real difference, from the standpoint of the undoctrinaire secularist, is not in anachronistic usages like the above, but in the tax exemption of church property. Here, if anywhere, the separation of state and church is clearly violated. This is a momentous issue not merely because the services of the state for which all citizens pay, religious and nonreligious, are being used to protect church property, but because in some communities, at a time when local governments find themselves being pressed by the necessity of finding a larger tax base, an appreciable source of tax revenue is being lost by growth in church property. This is not a new problem, but it is one which is becoming more acute with the years. It was recognized as long ago as 1875 by President Ulysses S. Grant, who, although not distinguished for his acumen in political and social affairs, nonetheless recognized the significance of the problem. In warning about the perils of tax exemption, he wrote:

> In a growing country where real estate enhances rapidly with time, as in the United States, there is scarcely a limit to the wealth that may be acquired by corporations, religious and otherwise. . . . I would suggest the taxation of *all* property equally, whether church or corporative, exempting only the last resting place of the dead, and possibly, with proper restriction, church edifices.

President Grant's warning is especially relevant in view of the growth of tax-exempt properties, held by the churches, that are unrelated to religious purposes. This warning has gone unheeded not only by Congress but by the Courts, which are apparently more concerned with the terrible persecution suffered by children subjected to the reading of some Bible verses. It is safe to say that in consequence of the totally unnecessary public furore resulting from

the Supreme Court's decisions in the prayer and
Bible-reading cases, which I shall discuss later, the
Supreme Court will *not* rule that tax exemption of
church property violates the First Amendment, if a
taxpayer's suit on this issue ever comes before it, in
order to prove that it is not hostile to religion as such.
Judging by the defensive tone of the judgment and
concurring opinions in the prayer and Bible-reading
cases, it will be surprising if in the future it grants
certiorari to cases of this kind.

Where a grave evil exists—or a clear evil even
when it is not grave—no statute of limitation
should be recognized on the moral necessity of its
abolition. Neither time nor custom can moderate
the abomination of religious persecution or discrimination. However, where we are not faced by religious persecution or discrimination, but only by
historic vestiges of a religiously oriented culture that
have no harmful effects on those who are nonreligious
or who do not share the dominant religion, but at
the worst produce occasional irritation or boredom,
it is needless zealotry to seek to extirpate them by
the exercise of state power. *Summa jus, summa injuria.*
Just as the quest for absolute justice sometimes
results in more evil and, in the end, less justice than
acceptance of the greatest amount obtainable, even
if it falls short of perfection, so the attempt by

excommunicatory legal decree to purge a culture of all public manifestations of the religion in which it has been cradled may create greater evils, even from the standpoint of an intelligent secularism, than reliance upon the eroding influences of scientific modernism, religious pluralism, and democratic education.

What must be resisted is any attempt to introduce a *new* and *fresh* religious exercise or reference into public educational or political life. If the federal government were to undertake to build a chapel for Congressmen to pray for Divine guidance, this would be a clear violation of the principle of religious neutrality. In 1954, when the pledge of allegiance to flag and country was revised by Congress in order to introduce the phrase "under God," this was a manifest and illegitimate intrusion of religion which should have been more widely contested than it was. Its meaning and motivation were obviously religious, and offensive to those patriots whose loyalty to the nation and to its democratic institutions is no more dependent upon God, if He exists, than upon Santa Claus. Fifty or a hundred years from now, if the Supreme Court rules out the use of the phrase as violating the First Amendment, the religious sensibilities of the nation will undoubtedly be outraged, particularly if the pledge and the reference to God is not mandatory. But although

74

Congress made no provision for any exemptions, the Supreme Court refused to review a New York State decision upholding the constitutionality of the religiously amended pledge.

It is amusing to observe Justice Brennan's attempt to discount the religious significance of the *revised* pledge of allegiance. To any ingenuous mind the revised pledge with its explicit reference to God is just as much a violation of the establishment clause as noncoerced prayer and Bible reading. According to Justice Brennan, however, the reference to God does not mean what it seems to say. It is a merely secular reference on the part of those who recite the pledge to the outcome of a purely historical research question about the origins of the United States! "The reference to divinity in the revised pledge of allegiance, for example, may [*sic*!] merely recognize the historical fact that our Nation was believed to have been 'under God.'"[9]

Why should students or anyone else be interested in the founders' religious beliefs rather than in their beliefs in the injustice of taxation without representation? Surely, the first was not as relevant as the second to the Revolutionary cause. George III was on just as good terms with the Divinity in 1776 as was George Washington. If Justice Brennan's

[9] See footnote 5, above.

observations seem strained and farfetched at this point, they compare favorably with the other justifications he and the other Justices offer for their decisions in *Engel v. Vitale* and *Abington School District v. Schempp*. To this we now turn.

V

Much Ado About Prayer and Bible Reading

"The way of life of a nation, *les mœurs*," writes Professor B. Namier, "cannot be transformed by an act of will, or an edict."[1] This is a half-truth; it is wholly true only when the act of will or an edict comes out of the blue, which it rarely does. Provided one is willing to pay the price for an edict, it can transform a nation, as the history of the Soviet Union shows. And where change has a more evolutionary pattern, laws and decrees can have a profound influence on developments. This is especially true of some United States Supreme Court opinions. Without Truman's executive order desegregating the armed forces and a whole series of state legislative actions directed against discrimination, it is not likely that the decision in *Brown v.*

[1] *Avenues of History* (London: Macmillan and Co., 1952), p. 4.

Topeka Board of Education would have been handed down in 1954. But who can doubt that this decision gave power and legitimacy to the civil rights movement and insured its ultimate triumph?

Decrees, whether by legislatures or Courts, can make the difference between the failure and success of a popular movement. Sometimes, however, by being ill-timed or supererogative, decrees may divide the community unnecessarily without strengthening the institutional democratic pattern in behalf of which they were issued. This seems to me to be the case with the Supreme Court opinions in the prayer and Bible-reading cases, which produced possibly the greatest outcry against the Supreme Court since the days of the Dred Scott decision.

Despite the intensity of the opposition and dire predictions concerning the decline of both religion and morals in America, the republic still stands. Nonetheless, if the perfervid religionists were hysterical in their reactions to the decisions of the Court— even liberals like Reinhold Niebuhr and Bishop Pike joined the chorus of denunciation—there was still something perverse about the judgment in these cases. It created a national issue where one did not exist before. It interfered with the processes of local compromise and accommodation which had so effectively eliminated offensive sectarian religious practices from public and educational life. It reached a new low, not only in argument but in the improvisation of fact on which the argument was presumably based. It unfortunately gave a new lease on life to the parochial school movement which exploited the Court decisions in resisting tendencies to liquidate religious divisiveness in education.

Before discussing the Supreme Court decisions, it is important to understand what the Court decided with respect to prayer and Bible reading in schools. It not only declared unconstitutional any state law making these practices *mandatory* in schools, to which no one could reasonably take exception; it outlawed these practices even where they were discretionary. That is to say, even where these practices had been adopted by a local school board after consultation with parent-teacher associations and other lay bodies, they were declared to be in violation of the anti-Establishment clause of the First Amendment. Further, even where explicit provision was made for the exemption of any or all children who had conscientious scruples against listening to these recitals and readings, this, too, was barred. The result was that in hamlets and towns in states like Vermont, in which a few verses of Bible reading had opened the school day in schools for more than a century, without any opposition to the practice ever having been recorded, teachers and parents awoke to discover that they had been violating the Constitution. The entire pattern of local and voluntary accommodation and compromise in which Protestant discrimination against Catholicism and Judaism had been moderated to the vanishing point, and in which religious practices in public life had dwindled into ritualistic significance, was swept aside by a flat taboo. Nowhere in the United States could a teacher read to a class a few verses from the Bible, except as an illustration in the course of a lesson on some specifically nonreligious subject, without breaking the law. Such a decision seems at first glance to be neither politically wise, nor educationally sound, nor dictated by the constitutional bar against an established church or religion.

Indeed, there is something irrepressibly comical in the solemn and labored effort to prove that an innocuous and "bland"—the adjective is Justice Brennan's—prayer, addressed not so much to the God of any recognized religion as To Whom It May Concern, or the reading of some Bible verses, is a manifestation of an established religion or a significant step towards establishment. Even the one-sentence prayer kindergarten children have lisped before eating their cookies has now been ruled a threat to the separation of church and state.

There are many reasons why the characterization of these practices as constituting an establishment of religion is, to put it mildly, invalid.

1. The ordinary-language rule for the employment of the phrase "established religion" or "established church" precludes its use as a designation of these innocuous practices, especially when they are not compulsory and students are exempt from participation. (Actually, so innocuous are these practices taken to be that some religious persons who uphold the Court's position argue that in the interest of a vital and healthy religion, the anemic measures objected to by the Court should be discontinued.) Anyone who attended American public schools fifty years ago in metropolitan centers of mixed population and religious faiths will recall that many more evidences of the Christian faith were then an integral part of the school curriculum than at the time of the Supreme Court decisions. The school day began not only with Bible reading but with Protestant hymns. Yet no one ever took them as signs of a religious establishment during these years. The proud boast of our text books, of our educational leaders and statesmen, was that no established religion existed in the United States, and that in the eyes of the state there were no second-class citizens—so characteristic of a community

which supported an established religion. Had anyone referred to the vestigial religious practices of
the schools as a sign of an established religion, he
would have been regarded as guilty of a plain abuse
of language.

2. Establishment at the time the Constitution was
adopted meant an established church. There was no
established religion without an established church
then or since. The fact that the term "religion"
rather than "church" is found in the first Amendment does not necessarily signify that a distinction
was recognized between the two, and that the
language of the Amendment was reaching out not
only to prevent church establishments on the federal
level, comparable to those on the state level, but
also to forestall any religious practice. Even today
in many contexts, including Supreme Court opinions,
the expressions "separation of church and state" and
"separation of religion and state" are used interchangeably. The same is true of the expressions
"establishment of religion" and "establishment of
church."

3. If practices like Bible reading and a general
prayer were sufficient to establish a church or
religion or constituted an important step towards
such establishment, then since these practices have
been in vogue for more than a hundred years, we

should be well along the road to the abolition of the principle of religious neutrality.

4. Those who consider *these* practices of admittedly minimal religious significance to be a definite threat of establishment dismiss the far more serious aid given by the state to organized religion through tax exemption and payment of the salaries of military chaplains as constitutionally protected. This judgment betrays a basic inconsistency in the conception of what constitutes an establishment. The contention that these latter practices, which more closely resemble the practices essential to establishment than the condemned prayer and Bible reading, are justified by the clause which guarantees "the free exercise of religion" is without warrant. Nondiscriminatory taxation of church property is not an abridgment of freedom of religion. It is false to say that religious institutions benefit from remission of taxes "in spite of rather than because of their religious character" and that they "simply share benefits which government makes generally available to educational, charitable, and eleemosynary groups."[2] The tax laws recognize the category of "the religious" as distinctly separable from the character of the educational or charitable as qualifying an

[2] This is Justice Brennan's claim in his concurring opinion in *Abington School District v. Schempp*, 374 U.S. 301 (1963).

institution for exemption from taxation. If a religious institution engaged in no educational or charitable activity whatsoever—and some do not—it would still be entitled under the law to tax exemption.

The same defective reasoning characterizes the justification of the state support of chaplains in the military forces and prisons. The argument that if the state conscripts a man from civilian life, or isolates him after he has committed a crime, it is an interference with his religious freedom unless he is provided an opportunity to worship proves too much or too little. It proves too much since, if it were taken seriously, it would require that the state undertake the cost of constructing churches and synagogues and mosques and pagodas for the plural religious needs of its conscripts. It proves too little because the state can easily provide the *opportunity* for various religious denominations to service their coreligionists without using tax money to subsidize their chaplains. There is a profound difference between giving a man an opportunity to practice his religion and underwriting its costs. Nor is there any doubt that most denominations would be willing to forgo this government subsidy and not insist on it as a precondition for their ministering to the faithful. Justice Brennan, who has taken upon himself the burden of making more persuasive the Court's decision on Bible reading in the public schools, is singularly unconvincing when he argues that it would be "hostility" towards religion and not "neutrality" were the *state* to refuse to provide chaplains and places of worship to the military. Among the features he lists as differentiating the "neutral" practice of state subsidy of chaplains from the biased practice of Bible reading is that "there is no element of coercion present . . . the soldier who declines the opportunities for worship would not ordinarily subject himself to the suspicion or obloquy of his peers." The school child, on the other hand, presumably is being coerced if he exercises his privilege of exemption.

We shall presently discuss this question as a *matter of fact* in some detail, but at this point we shall dwell on the significance the voluntary or involuntary character of an act has for our judgment of its legitimacy.

5. One of the necessary conditions of an established church or religion is that it enjoy some monopoly in respect to some religious practice which is prescribed for all or whose costs are borne by all. There could be no reasonable objection to any Court decision which outlawed any prescription of even a minimal religious nature in education or public life. The spirit of neutrality would be violated

if a witness, for example, were required to swear and could not affirm. But who can reasonably claim that the swearing of a witness or the prayer for Divine guidance which opens the sessions of our legislative assemblies, and which has about as much influence on the subsequent proceedings as the opening classroom prayer on the business of the school day, is the nose of the establishment camel in the tent of the free society? There is a difference, disregarded by the Court, between compelling and permitting. Were schools to attempt to *compel* all or any students to listen to a few verses from the Bible against their will, short shrift should be given to the enabling legislation. But a legislation which *permits* local option by the school board on condition that the right of exemption be scrupulously observed is something else again.

The Court argues that the fact that any and all students may be exempt from the provisions in question does not affect the *obligatory* character of the practice, and that even if no element of compulsion enters into the manner in which the provisions are carried out, it breaches the ironclad rule against an establishment of religion. In addition, the Court argues on independent grounds that despite the exemptions, coercion is indirectly involved, so that the provisions ruled out by the Court violate the constitutional safeguards of "freedom of religion." I shall examine the first point here, and the second in the following chapter.

The presupposition of our discussion is that we are dealing with a historical question to which common-sense observations are not irrelevant. I wish to repeat once more that were we founding a democratic community of plural religious faiths, there could be no justification for the introduction of even faintly devotional elements in state and school. But when we are dealing with the vestigial remains of a once strongly religious culture, it is the better part of common sense to rely on gradual processes of enlightenment to hasten the euthanasia of religious practices in public life rather than to arouse sleeping religious furies by legal interdiction. Common sense not only suggests this historical approach; it also enters in the recognition that the devotional exercises we are here discussing are devotional in a minimal sense, that they are no more devotional than other religious vestiges in public life which the Court is prepared to accept as constitutionally unobjectionable.

We must bear this approach in mind in order to meet a point made by Professor Paul Freund of the Harvard Law School, who has presented a much better case for the Supreme Court decisions in

Engel v. Vitale and *Abington v. Schempp* than any of the Justices. He argues that the mere fact that exemption from attendance is granted dissenters to the practice of prayer and Bible reading would hardly be a sufficient protection in all circumstances.

> The free exercise of religion includes the right to worship in one's accustomed way. Does it then follow that where a majority in a school are Jews or Catholics they may bring in a rabbi or priest to conduct full scale religious services every day, with a full panoply of ritual and insignia, giving the minority the privilege of absenting themselves? [3]

The short answer to this is: "Of course not!" If there were any danger of this, no one could today reasonably oppose the absolute taboos against the nonsectarian vestigial practices of prayer and Bible reading. This would be an extreme form of released time already outlawed by the Court in *McCollum v. Board of Education*.[4] If there were any historical danger that these full-blown religious practices would result from the recital of a one-sentence "bland" prayer or from a few Bible verses, it would

[3] *A Dialogue on Church and State* (unabridged addresses given at a conference on the meaning of the First Amendment, published by the Indiana Area of the Methodist Church, 1963), p. 7.
[4] 333 U.S. 203 (1948).

have manifested itself long ago. In some public schools such recitals have opened the school day for more than a century without religious flooding of the curriculum. Actually, the historical evidence points to the progressively greater secularization of the school curriculum. This is true even on the private college and university level. The compulsory chapel of the nineteenth century, without benefit of Court decisions, instead of becoming more and more religious in character has become less so, even when the requirement of attendance was dropped. Suppose someone were to argue against tax exemption of churches, not on the sufficiently valid ground that this is a clear violation of the principle of state neutrality as currently understood by the philosophy of democracy, but on the ground of the possible danger that the continuance of tax exemption might lead to the restoration of state-supported church-tithing. Would we not, in the absence of relevant evidence that there was any genuine danger of this happening, dismiss the notion as fanciful?

To be sure, the Court is not qualified to pass judgment on the *nice* details of what is religious and nonreligious, sectarian and nonsectarian. But from a broad point of view, it is already immersed in that kind of task already, not only in considering what constitutes religious grounds of conscientious

89

objection to military service, not only in exempting
certain kinds of solicitation of funds by "religious
organizations" from the scope of the mail-fraud
statutes, but in the very characterization of Bible
reading, despite claims to the contrary from super-
intendents of education, as devotional. It is an
intolerable legalism to pretend that the Court
cannot take judicial notice of obvious fact, that it
cannot distinguish between the celebration of Mass
in a public school and Bible reading. It is even worse,
as we shall see, to invent its facts whenever its
doctrinaire position is challenged by the results of
historic experience.

Once we drop the myth that the Court is applying
the First Amendment to current affairs according
to the meaning of the words as presumably understood by the Founding Fathers, and recognize that
the Court is really *legislating* in the light of what it
today considers wise or just or democratic, it is not
too much to expect some evidence of the common
sense and gumption which should never be absent
from the deliberation of legislators.

VI

The Issue of Coercion

It is very instructive to observe that when some of the Justices of the Supreme Court refer to sundry religious practices which could with as much justification be considered violations of the establishment clause of the First Amendment as prayer and Bible reading, they stress the fact that no element of coercion is involved. Justice Brennan, as we have seen, makes much of the absence of coercion when arguing that the state subsidy of chaplains is constitutional. Justice Douglas, before him, in approving released time for religious education in *Zorach v. Clauson*, distinguishes this practice from the released time condemned by the Court in *McCollum v. Board of Education*, on the ground that the instruction in the first case was optional and not marked by any coercion.

However, when the Justices assess the claim that

the exemption freely given to students who have
conscientious scruples to listening to Bible reading
makes the observance voluntary, they declare nonetheless that the establishment clause of the First
Amendment is clearly breached, even if the clause
concerning freedom of religion is not.

From an operational point of view, it could be
argued that where there is no abridgment of freedom
of religion in *any* sense, there is hardly much point in
protesting against an establishment. Historically,
establishment at the very least has always involved
some financial support by the state of some religious
observances. If the use of general tax money
for a religious observance disapproved of by some
citizen or group of citizens is construed as a restric-
tion upon their freedom, then it is analytically true
that an established religion violates the right of
religious freedom. Of course, an established religion
could restrict or limit religious freedom in many
other, and much more repressive, ways. But unless
one could make a case that in some fashion or other
some citizen's religious freedom is oppressively
affected by a religious establishment, the very concept of an establishment would represent an otiose
abstraction, or if not otiose, certainly not odious.
That case can easily be made on the basis of the
historical record. Within the protective shadow of

every established religion lurks the specter of persecution. At any rate, the two principles "free exercise of religion" and "opposition to establishment" seem to have gone together in the thinking of the architects of the Constitution. " 'Establishment' [or rather, anti-establishment] and 'free exercise,' " writes Mr. Justice Rutledge, dissenting in *Everson v. Board of Education*, "were correlative and coextensive ideas, representing only different facets of the single great and fundamental freedom."[1]

Whether historically accurate or not, this emphasis upon "the great and fundamental" ideal of freedom of religion must be our guiding principle in the present. Nor do the Justices of the Supreme Court really deny this. For despite the fact that the Court asserts that the establishment clause would be violated even in the absence of any evidence that nonobserving individuals have been coerced by the provisions for prayer and Bible reading, it insists that the coercion is present anyhow, exemption or no exemption.

A great deal is made of this point by both Justice Black and Justice Clark, who wrote the majority opinions in the prayer and the Bible-reading cases respectively, and by Justice Brennan. Now, on the face of it, it seems singularly implausible to assert

[1] *Everson v. Board of Education*, 330 U.S. 40 (1946).

that a child's religious freedom is being violated
when specific exemption is provided for him merely
on the request of his parents. We are here dealing
with questions of psychological fact that cannot be
deduced merely from legal, or abstract psychological,
principles. Once the facts in the case are challenged,
only inquiry can settle them. This is the whole
point of Justice Stewart's dissenting and much
neglected opinion in the Bible-reading cases. If there
is any element of coercion involved in the asking or
receiving of exemption from listening to prayer
and/or Bible reading, these practices should be
barred under the "free exercise" clause of the First
Amendment. About this there can be no dispute.
But how are we to find out? Some of the Justices
contend that coercion is built into the very nature
of the situation. Thus Justice Brennan writes in
answer to the assertion that no coercion is exercised
when practices are voluntary: "The answer is that
the excusal procedure itself *necessarily* operates in
such a way as to infringe the rights of free exercise
of those children who wish to be excused" (my
italics).[2] No actual evidence is given for believing
that the excusal procedure in this type of situation
necessarily infringes the rights of free exercise. What
is cited is evidence from some behavioral social

[2] 374 U.S. 288 (1963).

94

scientists concerning the susceptibility of students to various factors in the school environment. But if the influence of the teacher is considered among these factors, no determinate answer can be given. Justice Brennan is not the only one in the American judiciary, nor is the American judiciary alone, in believing that students would be intimidated by fear of the negative judgment of their peer groups were they to avail themselves of the exemptions legally provided. They write as if this is an inescapable inference requiring no confirmation. If this is an inescapable inference, why, then, did not the Court make it in *Zorach v. Clauson* when it approved released time for religious instruction? If anything, here was a more conspicuous and massive deviation from accepted peer group values than a discreet excusal procedure which allows exempt students to come to school a few minutes late, after the Bible verses have been read, if they wished. If the Court assumes that any exemption given to children automatically holds them up to the scorn and derision of their fellow students, then it would also follow that the children of Jehovah's Witnesses, exempt from giving the salute to the flag in *West Virginia Board of Education v. Barnette*[3] are being denied their rights under the "free exercise" clause of the

[3] 319 U.S. 624 (1943).

95

First Amendment, even when the excusal procedure is open to them. Should we therefore forbid the pledge of allegiance to the flag on the ground that it interferes with the religious freedom of the children of Jehovah's Witnesses? Or is the Supreme Court to rule that the pledge of allegiance to the flag, with or without the phrase "under God," has no religious element in it? But if the pledge is deemed without religious significance to those who object to it, then why the exemption to those who declared themselves conscientiously opposed to the practice on specifically religious grounds?

At this point I beg the reader's indulgence for a personal but not irrelevant reference. As a lifelong educator who began my career teaching in the elementary schools, and who has kept in touch with actual school practices not only through the educational careers of my children, but in virtue of my sustained interest in the theory and practice of education, I can safely make a generalization that will be confirmed by unprejudiced inquirers or by intelligent observers. This is that with respect to religion in the *public* schools, children are much more defensive towards, and tolerant of, religious differences than they are towards apparent differences in patriotic conviction and loyalty. Where country and flag are concerned, they are apt to develop a strong national fervor, and very often an aggressive and intolerant chauvinism. Whatever the causes of their different attitudes towards variations in religion and variations in patriotic orthodoxy, the difference is striking.

Indeed, as I reflect on my own experience and that of my classmates in the public schools of a Brooklyn slum in pre-World War I days, what stands out is our complete indifference to the religious atmosphere and trappings of Christianity so palpably present in the life of the school. Within a few years these religious anachronisms were to be almost completely eliminated, except for the Bible reading, without any conflict between the different religious and ethnic groups in the community. This gradual elimination of religious symbols and rituals followed unofficial representations by lay rather than religious organizations. But while they remained, the children, both Jewish and non-Jewish, had a thoroughly sophisticated attitude towards them. We sang Protestant hymns, not a word of which we put any stock in, with great fervor and enjoyment. We welcomed any religious celebration if only it meant a school holiday. On the walls of our classroom there hung religious pictures of various types; our favorite was one of Christians being thrown to the lions in the Roman arena. We both admired the Christians, so serene under the lions' paws, and felt a little sorry for the poor lions who had no Christians. The idea that our religious freedom was being violated even though there was no provision for exemption from any religious exercises would have been hilarious. Except for some of the young prigs, the class would sooner have had a Bible lesson than a test!

Most of these religious practices had disappeared from the New York school system ten years later when I taught in the public elementary and high schools of the same area. There was still Bible reading in the classrooms and general assemblies. Although these readings were not commented upon, they served as splendid illustrative material for subsequent lessons in English, history, civics, and dramatics. Effective educational use could be made of Bible reading; and if someone had asked—which never happened—if the Bible stories were true, the reaction would have been the same as if a child had asked whether a poem were true. So far as I could judge, the children no more took literally what they heard than did Paul Tillich! In those days the state of parochial Jewish education was such that most of the Jewish children who were compelled to read the Bible in Hebrew, after public school hours, until they were confirmed at the age of thirteen, understood the Bible properly only when they heard it read in English.

98

Although I do not wish to prejudge matters on the basis of an experience that may not have been representative, my conviction is that if provisions for exemption from Bible reading had existed in the early twenties and had been invoked by any child, there would have been no hostility whatsoever from his peer group. It is even possible that he might have been regarded as a "serious type"—one of the multiple elite groups recognized in a normal class. More likely, such a child would have been regarded with sympathy as one of those children who was being "victimized" by his parents' excessive concern with what was going on in the classroom—except that *his* parents were fussy about religion rather than about wearing rubbers during recess or not sitting in a draft.

Had there been the slightest sign that students regarded with hostility anyone who asked for exemption, as a teacher it would have been easy to explain and make acceptable the whole practice as part of America's proud tradition of religious tolerance. Dean Erwin Griswold of the Harvard Law School seems to me to be perfectly justified in arguing on educational grounds that the practice of exemption today could serve as a persuasive lesson in civil rights. It is hard to believe that under such circumstances the children, or rather, the parents

99

whose consciences object to their "being exposed to reading the King James version of the Bible," would forgo invoking the privilege open to them.

The reason offered by the father of the children in the Abington schools who was a plaintiff in the case that reached the Supreme Court, for *not* requesting his children to be excused from hearing the Bible read—something he could very well have done—will hardly bear examination. He contends that had he done so, his children would have been labelled "odd balls" by their teachers and fellow students. They might have been regarded as "atheists," even "communists!"

This explanation is questionable on its very face, aside from the gratuitous charge about the attitude of his children's teachers. Fearful of making his children conspicuous by invoking a perfectly legal exemption, this parent makes them a thousand times more conspicuous! He brings a legal action that puts his children in the national limelight, an action that can be construed as an effort to *prevent* his children's friends and associates from listening to Bible verses in the school. Which action is more likely to make Mr. Schempp's children appear "odd balls" and to generate resentment against them among their peer groups—the invocation by the children of an exemption that invades no one else's right to listen or not listen, or the bringing of a legal action which would make *Mr. Schempp's* conscience the bar to the right of millions to have their children listen to Bible verses?

The reaction of other children to the invocation of the legal right of exemption is at most problematic. The reaction of these children to the suit that would deny them what, rightly or wrongly, they believe to be *their* religious freedom could be anticipated. Were the parent in the case sincerely concerned only about the religious freedom of his children, he would have invoked the legal exemption. Had subsequent embarrassment of his children then resulted from the reactions of their teachers and peer group to a point where their religious freedom was being prejudiced, he could then have brought his suit.

That it is unlikely the petitioner would have had evidence of discrimination is suggested by the experience of the parent in the other case that reached the Court from Baltimore, Maryland. Here, too, the law provided that children could be excluded from hearing the Bible read or the Lord's Prayer recited on request of the parent. But in this case, in contradistinction to the previous one, the parent requested excusal and it was granted. The petition of the plaintiff does *not* contend that the invocation of the excusal procedure resulted in discrimination against or ridicule or harassing of the student in question by either the teacher or the student's classmates.

This does not settle the matter; it leaves the matter open, and makes the dissenting opinion of Justice Stewart highly pertinent. Before turning to it, I cannot forbear from commenting on Justice Douglas' remarkably sober judgment on this point which contrasts so strongly both with some of the judicial and some of the lay pronunciamentos on the subject.

In his concurring judgment in *Abington v. Schempp*, Mr. Justice Douglas argues that Bible reading violates the establishment clause, even if the practice is purely voluntary. One of his main grounds is that state funds are being used to finance it. "Through the mechanism of the State, all the people are being required to finance a religious exercise that only some of the people want and that violates the sensibilities of others." If the cost of the exercise were a valid reason for opposing it, it would hold even if *all* the people wanted a few verses of the Bible read in school. As to how many objected, the evidence shows very few; and with respect to these few the chief question, it seems to me, is whether they are under *coercion*. For the financial burden upon the community in reading the Bible is *minimal*. Were the practice discontinued, there would be no saving of school expense, since the Bible would still be a part of the class or school library anyhow, whether it was read or not as an opening exercise. Actually, there is less financial burden on the community in the reading of the Bible than in the official supervision of the practices of released time which Justice Douglas approved in *Zorach v. Clauson*. It would be surprising to find that any item of the school budget was dropped when Bible reading was eliminated from the curriculum. What in the world does Justice Douglas imagine the classroom teacher would do with the five minutes or less he saved by not reading the Bible? The financial saving would be nonexistent.

But in scrabbling around for supporting reasons for his concurrent opinion, Justice Douglas must be awarded full credit for recognizing that the Court is not confronted by the issue of compulsion or coercion.

> In these cases we have no coercive religious exercises aimed at making the students conform. The prayers announced are not compulsory, though some may think they have that indirect effect because the non-conformist student may be induced to participate for fear of being called an "odd ball." But that coercion, if it be present, has not been shown . . . .

This is all the more remarkable because, as Justice Douglas' past opinions have shown, he legitimately invites the rebuke a member of the English Long Parliament once addressed to a colleague: "You will shout 'Fire! Fire!' be it in Noah's flood!" All one need do is read his dissenting opinion in *Adler v. Board of Education*.[4] *A propos* of a foolish New York statute laying down certain procedures to be followed in reporting the membership of teachers in subversive organizations, Justice Douglas predicted in spine-chilling rhetoric a regime of terror in the schools suggestive of Orwell's *1984*.

Justice Douglas' restraint in his concurrent opinion contrasts very favorably with a great many hysterical interpretations of the significance of the Court's decision in the Bible-reading cases emanating both from those who approved and those who disapproved. Among the latter, the fantastic exaggerations of the rightwing of the Catholic Church and of the southern fundamentalists and reactionaries could have been anticipated. According to them, this decision, as well as the decision in *Engel v. Vitale*, meant that a philosophy of militant secularism hostile to all manifestations of religion in both public and private life had become the reigning political orthodoxy of the United States. Bishop Fulton J. Sheen, who

[4] 342 U.S. 485 (1952).

had argued in effect during the Second World War that if one begins with Luther and Protestantism, one will end with Hitler and Naziism, declared: "Our schools are now officially put on the same level as the Communist schools."[5] A pity that the Reverend Bishop has never observed what takes place in Communist schools.

What was more shocking was to read the character of the support of the Court decision from some liberal churchmen and organizations. One becomes immunized after some decades to drivel issued by southern Bourbons and segregationists. But when liberals associate the Negro drive for freedom from the degrading practices of political, social, economic, and religious discrimination, with the end of Bible reading in the public schools, when they suggest that those who wish to retain the uncoerced practice of Bible reading and/or prayer are of the same kidney as those who deny the humanity of the Negro, it leaves one aghast. Nonetheless, this is the burden of the *Letter from the General Council to the Members of the United Presbyterian Church in the United States of America,* which received widespread circulation. The letter states:

When children are forced by law, intimidation,

[5] Quoted by M. R. Konvitz in *Expanding Liberties* (New York: Viking Press, 1966), p. 45.

custom, or other pressures, to express or accept a faith that is neither theirs nor that of their parents, their humanity is denied. When men are turned away from God's house because of the color of their skin, their humanity is denied.[6]

This irresponsible coupling by the General Council of the United Presbyterian Church of those who saw no force or intimidating pressure in measures which even Justice Douglas declared free of coercion, with the southern red-neck fanatics of segregation is uncharitable, un-Christian, and, what is worst of all, unintelligent. It is surprising that the General Council, which has sternly disapproved of guilt by association, did not couple disapproval of the Supreme Court's decision with Hitler's extermination of the Jews! It is not altogether irrelevant that *before* the Court decisions, the General Council of the United Presbyterian Church did *not* call for an absolute proscription of all Bible-reading and prayer exercises in public schools. How could it have been so blind to an evil comparable to the moral abomination of segregation? If the Court had not granted certiorari to these cases or if Justice Stewart had spoken for the Court, would the General Council have issued its letter?

[6] "Of Judgment and Reconciliation," *Presbyterian Life,* December 1963, p. 6.

Justice Stewart did *not* vote to uphold the constitutionality of the disputed statutes. He was the only Justice who felt that the Court should have suspended judgment on the central issue by remanding the cases for further hearing in a quest for additional evidence. On this point it seems to me that his position is unexceptionable. The Court should have followed his lead here, even if it could not accept his strange identification of a strict neutrality of the state towards religion in public life with the religion of secularism.

Some of Justice Stewart's words might well be taken as the classic formulation of the American credo concerning the relation between religion and state.

> What our Constitution indispensably protects is the freedom of each of us to be Jew or agnostic, Christian or atheist, Buddhist, or Free Thinker, to believe or disbelieve, to worship or not worship, to pray or keep silent, according to his own conscience, uncoerced and unrestrained by government.[7]

A ringing and noble sentence! But let us not read more into it than it says. There is nothing in it that *requires* that we allow in the *public* sector of experience equal time, equal provision, equal opportunity to profess or not to profess allegiance to the religious

[7] 374 U.S. 319–320 (1963).

doctrines, belief in which defines to some, salvation, and to others, superstition. Sufficient only is that in the *private* sector, all are equally privileged to believe and say whatever they please.

Nevertheless, even Justice Stewart, despite his insight, is on untenable ground in writing that "if religious exercises are held to be an impermissible activity in schools, religion is placed at an artificial and state-created disadvantage." But why? A child's life is not so completely determined by the five hours of his school experience that, absent religious practices, he is forever immune to the benefits of religious teaching *after* school hours. Suppose the American Society for the Advancement of Atheism were to make a comparable argument! Suppose its spokesman asserted that unless atheist children learned from hearing or reading proper atheist tracts in school about Biblical deception—incest, murder, rape, and foul play—they would be handicapped in learning about the good life subsequently. The absurdity of either argument lies on its face.

Since we must live with our history, let us try to do so with a sense of humor and proportion and without flaming absolutes, without outraging the local pieties unless these are clearly evil. There are many regions of the country in which outlawing

these inconsequential religious exercises has produced great distress, a feeling that religion itself is
being persecuted, and even calls for flagrant dis-
obedience. I call these exercises inconsequential
from the point of view of serious infraction of the
establishment clause, but they are not inconsequential from the point of view of the memory,
sentiment, and emotional ties bound up with them.
It is to be hoped that the good sense of officials will
save us the spectacle of federal marshals dragging
teachers out of classrooms to prevent them from
violating the establishment clause by intoning the
Lord's Prayer or by reciting some Biblical verses.

After all, what was gained by the Court's decisions? Who will argue, in the light of the religious
practices in public life left standing, that *theoretically*
the position of the Court is clearer today than it was
before? The very intensity of the opposition to the
Court's decisions in these cases may make the Court
more wary in the future from estopping much more
serious breaches in the principle of religious neutrality. There is a danger that a way will be found
to aid parochial religious schools indirectly by
presenting federal aid as if it were aid primarily to
the child or students in those schools and not to the
schools themselves.

From my own educational point of view, the

weightiest reason for doubting the wisdom of the Court decisions in *Engel v. Vitale* and *Abington v. Schempp* is that they will lead to an extension of the parochial school system. At a time when there is evidence that the parochial school system is on the defensive because of the great economic burdens it imposes on its sponsors, and because of the growth of the philosophy of democratic education, the Court decisions have acted as a welcome and powerful shot in the arm. They have enabled defenders of the parochial school system to argue falsely but effectively that the public schools are hostile to religion, and re-enforced the views of religious fundamentalists opposed to any kind of secular education.

The parochial school system—Catholic, Protestant, and Jewish—is undoubtedly constitutional, but I regard it as *educationally* unsound. To separate large sections of our youth from each other in their most formative period is to breed latent, and sometimes not so latent, hostility among them. The liberalization of some of the religious rituals may somewhat mitigate this hostility, but so long as religious instruction can be given after school hours, there is no educational justification for separating children every day from each other on the basis of their religious differences. The public school system—which one defender of the parochial school system once characterized as "*Our Public Enemy Number One*"—helped to forge a united nation. Anything which weakens it weakens the nation. The parochial school systems in many communities have weakened the public school and, indirectly, the nation. Because of the financial burden of the parochial schools, in many communities where patrons of parochial schools constitute a minority, the public schools have been starved and their educational possibilities frustrated. The remedy is certainly not to make public money available to parochial schools. This would have calamitous results. Every religious sect, in order to insulate its children from too intimate contact with the children of adherents of other religions and of nonbelievers, in order to keep them in the fold, would set up its own parochial schools at public expense. When they are frank, the advocates of parochial school education imply that religious values pervade the entire curriculum of studies. Although one may legitimately doubt this—there is no such thing, strictly speaking, as Christian geometry or Jewish geography or Catholic chemistry or biology—what is meant is that religion plays its role in the way these subjects are taught, in the illustrations used and practical deductions drawn.

Since the Supreme Court decisions, the prospects have greatly lessened that Catholic parochial schools will surrender their charges to the public schools. Among Protestant groups, which have hitherto been ardent supporters of the American public school, surprising strength has developed for Protestant—and not merely Lutheran—parochial schools. Bishop Fred P. Corson, president of the World Methodist Council, has declared that there has been "considerable sentiment expressed by Protestants in favor of Protestant parochial schools since the Supreme Court prayer ban decision."[8]

On pragmatic grounds which are also grounds of first principles in education, I should sooner prefer to have all students in one school system, freely congregating with each other, even at the price of a brief, uncoerced, uncommented-upon daily Bible reading and/or prayer, than to have two separate systems—one secular and one religiously oriented. Whatever the shortcomings of the secular school are, they do not stem from intellectual timidity. And whatever the virtues of parochial schools, they do not encourage the acquisition of those habits of critical and independent thought that may imperil the sanctities of faith. Fraternity, equality of opportunity, variety of educational experiences within a comprehensive curriculum, social democracy, and,

[8] *A Dialogue on Church and State* (Indianapolis: Indiana Methodist Press, 1963), p. 40.

last and least, economy and efficiency are better furthered by a common public school system that allows for religious instruction after school hours and off school premises than by an educational system which is fractured into two parts.

Religious conflict may sometimes cripple the functioning of a democratic community as effectively as class war. Today in the United States the only area of life in which religious differences threatens to upset the balanced tensions of political life is in education, particularly in the northeastern states. Whatever tendencies were struggling to develop in Catholic circles to surrender the parochial school system and let it be absorbed gradually by the public school system have withered away in consequence of the Court's recent decisions. As educational costs mount, we can anticipate additional and more desperate efforts to get public funds for parochial school purposes under the general formula of public welfare. The same reasoning which legitimized hot lunches for children and the underwriting of their transportation costs will be invoked for other aspects of education in parochial schools. It requires only a few new appointments to the Court in years to come, given the present state of constitutional law, to open up new sources of public support for private religious schools.

On the other hand, some doctrinaire secularists, on the principle that a half-loaf is worse than none, seem to be opposed to all forms of "shared time" between public and parochial schools. "Shared time" differs from objectionable "released time" in that pupils from parochial schools are permitted to attend public schools to study certain secular subjects under public school teachers and on public school premises. Instead of welcoming this opportunity to have students from the parochial schools mix with the students from the public schools, and devising methods by which this can be furthered, some secularists have opposed the entire idea of "shared time" as merely another method of surreptitiously supporting the parochial schools. Of course, some proposed schemes of "shared time" are obviously nothing but emergency measures for the economic relief of parochial schools too poor to equip themselves with laboratories in science. But whatever the motives behind the current willingness of parochial schools to accept proposals for "shared time," enlightened public school educators can implement the program in such a way that all children profit educationally from the experience. It is essential to mix the classes so that pupils from both systems study together, a difficult but not insuperable task of programming. Once undertaken in the proper spirit and with appropriate safeguards, the advantages may be such that the parochial schools in the end may be willing to function primarily as Sunday religious schools to those who wish to attend, leaving to the American public school system everything else. If we then lavish upon public education the concern, energy, money, and devotion which a need of such transcendent significance for democracy requires, we may usher in a new and golden age of American education.

Index

Abington v. Schempp, 16, 76, 83 n., 88, 100 ff., 110
Abortion, 20, 34, 36, 39
Adler v. Board of Education, 104
Aristotle, 18
Arnold, Matthew, 35
Atheism, 47, 108

Baltimore, Maryland, 101
Barth, Karl, 19
Bible, 18
Bible reading, v, vii, 8, 16, 22 ff., 45–46, 67 ff., 72 f., 75, 78 ff., 82, 85, 88, 90 ff., 97 ff., 103 ff., 109, 112
Bill of Rights, 18, 31
Birth control, 20, 33, 36, 39
Black, Justice, 31, 93
Blaine, James G., 49
Bonaparte, Napoleon, 48
Book of Common Prayer, 28
Brennan, Justice, 17, 67, 75, 80, 83 n., 84, 91, 93 ff.
Brown v. Topeka Board of Education, 62, 77–78

Cavell, Edith, 54
Chapel, compulsory, 89
Chaplains, military, 44, 68, 83 ff., 91
China, Communist, 54
Church, established, 28, 59, 64 ff., 81 ff., 85, 92 f., 102, 109; and state, vi f., 6 f., 12 ff., 16, 21, 59, 63 f., 71, 107
Church of England, 28
Civil rights, 11, 78, 99
Civil Rights Act of 1875, 62
Clark, Justice, 16, 64, 93
Coercion, 91 ff., 102 f., 106
Colleges, secularization of, 89
Communism, 51 ff., 105
Conscientious objection, 89–90
Corson, Fred P., 112
Crime, 40
Cults, 9, 70–71

Decalogue, 40
Declaration of Independence, 64

INDEX

Decrees, 78
Democracy, 11 ff., 23 f., 51, 53, 55, 60, 63
Denominations, 10
Dewey, John, 4, 15, 35
Discrimination, 73, 77
Divine, Father, 57
Divine Right of Kings, 14
Divorce, 20, 33–34, 37 f.
Douglas, Justice, 16 f., 22 ff., 91, 102 ff., 106

Education, 11, 23 ff., 34, 54 f., 63, 69, 74
Engel v. Vitale, 76, 88, 104, 110
Equality, human, 14–15
Ethics, 25 f.
Euthanasia, 20, 36
Everson v. Board of Education, 93

Fascism, 51
Feudalism, 14
Figgis, John N., 20
Founding Fathers, 15, 25, 64 f., 67, 90
Fraud, 56 f.
Free society, definition of, 10 ff.; *see also* Democracy
Freedom, 29; *see also* Religious freedom
Freund, Paul, 87
Fundamentalists, 104, 110

George III, 75
Germany, Nazi, 54

Goldberg, Justice, 45–46
Grant, Ulysses S., 72
Griswold, Erwin, 99

Harlan, Justice, 62
Herberg, Will, 51
Hitler, Adolf, 105 f.
Holmes, Justice O. W., 7
Hume, David, 35
Hutchins, Robert, 34

Ingersoll, Robert, 48

Jackson, Justice, 69
Jefferson, Thomas, 44, 50, 64 f.
Jehovah's Witnesses, 95 f.
Jewish children, 97 f.
Judaeo-Christian tradition, 13 f.

Kant, Immanuel, 32
Kierkegaard, Sören, 33

Law, 20, 26
Lippmann, Walter, 15
Long Parliament, 104
Luther, Martin, 105
Lutheran schools, 112

McCollum v. Board of Education, 68, 88, 91
Madison, James, 44, 50, 64 f.
Majority rule, 11, 64
Marriage, 20, 37; monogamic, 18, 56; plural, 32, 55

Marx, Karl, 59
Mayflower Compact, 64
Metternich, 48
Military service, exemption from, 44, 53, 90
Minorities, 64
Minors, employment of, 55
Monopolies, 11
Morality, 10, 32 ff., 40, 52, 55
Mormons, 56

Namier, B., 77
National anthem, 70
Negroes, 62, 105
Neutrality, state, 27, 31, 33, 36 f., 41, 43 ff., 50, 83, 85, 89, 107, 109
New York State, 98, 104
Niebuhr, Reinhold, 78
1984, 104
Northwest Ordinance, 25

Oaths, 70
Orwell, George, 13, 104

Parliament, 28, 104
Parochial schools, 22, 68 f., 79, 98, 109 ff.
Paul, Saint, 14
Persecution, 73, 93
Pike, James A., 78
Planned parenthood, 36
Plato, 32
Pledge of allegiance, 74 f., 95 f.

Plessy v. Ferguson, 62
Prayer in public schools, v, vii, 8, 22 ff., 67 ff., 73, 75, 78 ff., 82, 88, 91, 93 f., 101, 105 f., 109, 112
Prisons, 84
Protestantism, 105, 112
Public school system, vi–vii, 110 ff.
Pure Food and Drug Administration, 56

Reich, Wilhelm, 56
Released time, 22, 68 f., 88, 91, 95, 103, 114
Religion, definition of, 8–10; influence of, 20, 48 ff.
Religious freedom, 27 ff., 37, 55, 65, 83, 93
Roman Catholic Church, 104, 111, 113
Rutledge, Justice, 93

Santayana, George, 48, 53
Scott, Dred, 78
Secularism, 44 ff., 51 ff., 60, 74, 107, 114
Segregation, 62, 105 f.
Shared time, 114
Sheen, Fulton J., 104–105
Sin, 38–40
Slavery, 14, 18, 40, 60
Socrates, 4
Soviet Union, 54, 77
Stalinism, 19

State, *see* Church and state
Stewart, Justice, 94, 102, 106 ff.
Stoic philosophy, 14
Subversive organizations, 104
Suicide, 20
Sunday closing laws, 21

Tax exemption, 44, 68 f., 71 ff., 83, 89
Theology, 12 ff.
Tillich, Paul, 98
Totalitarianism, 51
Toynbee, Arnold, 9
Truman, Harry S., 77
Twain, Mark, 32

United Presbyterian Church, 105 f.
United States Congress, 6, 8, 72, 74 f.; of 1787, 25
United States Constitution, 60 ff., 93, 107; First Amendment, 8, 22, 27 f., 31 f., 62, 66 f., 70, 73 f., 79 f., 82, 90 ff.,

96; Fourteenth Amendment, 62, 67
United States Supreme Court, v ff., 6 ff., 16 ff., 21 ff., 26, 41, 45, 50, 61, 63, 67, 69, 72 ff., 77 ff., 81 f., 85 ff., 91, 93, 95 f., 101 ff., 105 ff., 109 ff.

Vaccination, 55
Vermont, 79

Warren, Chief Justice, 6, 25
Washington, George, 75
Weiss, Jonathan, 57 n.
Welfare, social, 18, 52, 113
West Virginia Board of Education v. Barnette, 95
Williams, Roger, 64
Wittgenstein, Ludwig, 5
World Methodist Council, 112

Zorach v. Clauson, 16, 68 f., 91, 95, 103